MOM, INC.

MOM, INC.

*The Essential Guide to Running
a Successful Business From Home*

Meg Mateo Ilasco & Cat Seto

CHRONICLE BOOKS
SAN FRANCISCO

Library of Congress Cataloging-in-Publication Data:

Ilasco, Meg Mateo.

   Mom, Inc. : the essential guide to running a successful business from home / Meg Mateo Ilasco, Cat Seto.

     p. cm.

   ISBN 978-1-4521-0121-7 (pbk.)

   1. Home-based businesses. 2. Branding (Marketing) 3. Internet marketing. 4. Parenting. I. Seto, Cat. II. Title.

   HD62.38.I43 2012

   658.0412—dc22

                                        2011011418

Manufactured in China

Designed by *Meg Mateo Ilasco*

AdSense, Blogger, Google and Youtube are registered trademarks of Google Inc. Airstreamer is a registered trademark of Thor Tech, Inc. Akismet and Wordpress are registered trademarks of Automattic, Inc. Amazon is a registered trademark of Amazon Technologies, Inc. American Apparel is a registered trademark of American Apparel, Inc. American Express OPEN is a registered trademark of American Express Marketing & Development Corp. Anthropologie is a registered trademark of U.O. Merchandise Inc. Authorize.net is a registered trademark of Cybersource Corp. Babies"R"Us is a registered trademark of Geoffrey, LLC. Big Cartel is a registered trademark of Indie Labs, LLC. BlackBerry is a registered trademark of Research in Motion Ltd. BlogHer is a registered trademark of BlogHer, LLC. Bugaboo is a registered trademark of Royalty Bugaboo GmbH Corp. CaféMom is a registered trademark of CMI Marketing, Inc. Chronicle Books is a registered trademark of Chronicle Books LLC. Count Me In for Women's Economic Independence and Make Mine a Million $ Business are registered trademarks of Count Me In For Women's Economic Independence. Cozi is a registered trademark of Cozi Group Inc. Dean & Deluca is a registered trademark of Dean & DeLuca Brands, Inc. EcoLogo is a registered trademark of TerraChoice Group, Inc. ENK Children's Club is a registered trademark of ENK International, LLC. Emory is a registered trademark of Emory University. Etsy is a registered trademark of Etsy, Inc. Evernote is a registered trademark of Evernote Corp. Excel and PowerPoint are registered trademarks of Microsoft Corp. Facebook is a registered trademark of Facebook, Inc. FedEx is a registered trademark of Federal Express Corp. Flickr is a registered trademark of Yahoo! Inc. Green Seal is a registered trademark of Green Seal, Inc. HootSuite is a registered trademark of Hootsuite. Kodak is a registered trademark of Eastman Kodak Co. Media, Inc. Illustrator and Photoshop are registered trademarks of Adobe Systems Inc. J.Crew is a registered trademark of J. Crew Int'l, Inc. LinkedIn is a registered trademark of LinkedIn Corp. LogMeIn is a registered trademark of LogMeIn, Inc. Lucky magazine and Cookie magazine are registered trademarks of Advance Magazine Publishers. M&M is a registered trademark of Mars, Inc. Meetup is a registered trademark of Meetup, Inc. MySpace is a registered trademark of MySpace Inc. Oeuf is a registered trademark of Oeuf, LLC. Paper Mart is a registered trademark of Frick Paper Co. Peachtree is a registered trademark of Sage Software, Inc. Pinterest is a registered trademark of Cold Brew Labs, Inc. Playtime is a registered trademark of Picaflor, Inc. QuickBooks is a registered trademark of Intuit, Inc. Rolodex is a registered trademark of Berol Corp. Roxy is a registered trademark of Quiksilver Americas, Inc. Spoonflower is a registered trademark of Spoonflower, Inc. Squarespace is a registered trademark of Squarespace, Inc. TweetDeck is a registered trademark of TweetDeck, Inc. Twitter is a registered trademark of Twitter, Inc. U.S. Postal Service is a registered trademark of the United States Postal Service. Uline.com is a registered trademark of Uline, Inc. UPS is a registered trademark of United Parcel Service of America, Inc. VeriSign is a registered trademark of VeriSign, Inc. Whole Foods is a registered trademark of Whole Foods Market, Inc. Wordtracker is a registered trademark of Rivergold Associates Ltd. Yahoo! is a registered trademark of Yahoo! Inc.

10 9 8 7 6 5 4 3 2 1

Chronicle Books LLC

680 Second Street

San Francisco, California 94107

www.chroniclebooks.com

TO OUR MOTHERS,

Dely Mateo and Jenny Seto

You are the inspiration behind this book. We are ever
grateful for your love, support, and belief in our goals
as both moms and entrepreneurs.

CONTENTS

BECOMING A MOTHER IS A RITE OF PASSAGE. Suddenly your world takes on new meaning, new chaos, and a new lens through which to view your priorities, career, and life goals. Perhaps being on maternity leave has allowed you to step away from the traditional workplace and you've had time to wonder, "How will I find child care when it's time to go back to work? Will it be hard to be away from the baby?" More and more, mothers are thinking of alternative careers that will allow them to stay at home and spend more time raising their kids. For many, this alternative career is an opportunity to pursue an artistic business, a dream they've been mulling over for years.

But the notion to start a business doesn't always come so early in motherhood. Plenty of women are driven by a need for a new order—a desire to revisit or develop a creative outlet that lets them express their individuality outside of the land of school calendars, padded play-grounds, and antibacterial gel. Maybe you've had a personal epiphany and have realized that you can take the woman out of the design firm, but you can't take the design firm out of the woman—and freelancing is calling your name. Or perhaps the deep bond that you have formed with your children has led you to yearn for something more personal, more creative as your livelihood—like decorating cakes to mark the milestones in people's lives. Whatever path has led you here, we want to tell you that starting a creative business while balancing the respon-sibilities of motherhood is absolutely doable and can be a profitable and successful venture.

You are likely to have an undeniable desire for an artistic outlet that goes beyond the weekend craft project. You'll discover that we, as well as the inspiring moms profiled in this book—from product designer and blogger to store owner and wedding photographer—have experienced different twists and turns along the road to transforming our desires into reality. We hope to inspire you and inform your own journey while showing you some creative, home-based business options—such as launching a blog, setting up a creative service, making and selling a product, or starting an online shop. From there we advise you on the nuances of each of these types of businesses, such as how to source your products, develop a winning portfolio, get the word out through

 You are likely to have an undeniable desire for an artistic outlet that goes beyond the weekend craft project.

social networking, and score publicity. And all of this advice is offered from the perspective of mothers who must juggle it all: clients, projects, schedules, child care, and family.

No doubt, the difficulties on the path to success are naturally going to be compounded by the challenges of working with one foot in the mother world and another in the business world. You will discover exactly how much you are capable of—and you'll be pleasantly surprised to find out that you are capable of more than you thought possible. You are making a concerted effort to pursue a lifestyle choice that takes you away from the corporate office and roots you at the center of your passions: family and creativity. You'll soon find yourself reaping the rewards of your new life: being creative in your day, taking ownership of pivotal decisions in business, and having the flexibility and freedom to be with your family. And, although your days will be one whirlwind after another, we hope that you'll soon agree with us that being an entrepreneurial mom gives you the best of both worlds.

the ENTREPRENEURIAL MOM

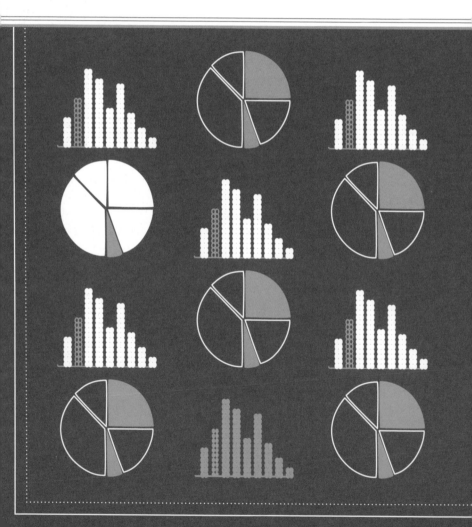

Motherhood often serves as a CATALYST FOR CHANGE in a woman's life—and for a growing number of women it's also become a siren call to start a business. Whether you're toying with the idea of STARTING A HOME-BASED BUSINESS so you can spend more time with your children, or you have more free time to PURSUE CREATIVE CAREER INTERESTS now that your little ones are in school—know that when you combine business with children, things will get messy. You will need to be a master multi-tasker—even more than you already are. Though you'll be doing A LOT OF JUGGLING, the biggest perks will be having a creative out-let and the flexibility to SHAPE YOUR CAREER AND FAMILY LIFESTYLE. In this chapter, we'll give you a taste of what it means to mix business and motherhood.

ARE YOU READY TO BE AN ENTREPRENEUR?

The truth is, pregnancy and entrepreneurship have a lot of similarities. For one thing, you don't fully understand what you've gotten yourself into until you're knee deep in diapers or profit and loss statements. You'll spend untold hours nurturing, molding, grooming, cleaning, and spending money on both your babies—your newborn and your new business. You will also experience many of the same emotions as you deal with both: happiness, frustration, disappointment, and glowing pride.

As mothers, we have limited quantities of resources, time, and energy—so we need to choose our commitments carefully. Obviously, a business is a huge investment and there's no getting around it: You will spend a lot of time on your new venture. When it takes off, you'll dedicate even more hours to it. But you can find a balance and make it all work. Remember that balance doesn't have to mean spending an equal amount of time on

 You'll spend untold hours nurturing, molding, grooming, cleaning, and spending money on both your babies—your newborn and your new business.

everything—there just isn't enough time in the day for that. It does mean that all parties should be satisfied in a relatively equal way—which may mean unplugging at the end of your workday to spend some quality hours with your family before they sleep.

Anyone can be an entrepreneur, and it's never too late (or too early) to be one. You certainly don't need to have a business degree (between the two of us, we have degrees in psychology and English). All you need is a dream, a plan, an abundance of determination and stamina, and above all, a firm belief in yourself. It also helps to be endowed with a few entrepreneurial characteristics. If you find that you have a few, if not all, of the following traits, then you've already got the makings of a creative mom entrepreneur:

Passion. You'd rather stay at home making a small army of crocheted elephants than spend a night out on the town with your girlfriends. Or your husband counts your camera as one of your children because it's always hanging on to your neck. This means you're passionate about your creative outlet. For the creative entrepreneur, her business is not just a job—it's a core part of her life. It's one of the reasons she's excited to get up in the morning and one of the last thoughts in her mind before she sleeps.

Attention to detail. Making cupcakes for your daughter's third-grade class caused you to borrow two books on icing techniques, purchase multipattern cupcake wrappers, and take a trip to the flea market for a milk-glass cake pedestal. You're detail oriented. Caring about everything connected to your business, no matter how small, will resonate with people and can make them loyal to your company.

Multitasking skills. Mothers are natural pros at interchanging tasks: We throw in the laundry while waiting for the pot to boil or pay bills online while on hold with the doctor's office. Thankfully, this talent for spinning plates can be applied to business tasks as well.

Decisiveness. When you have a four-year-old doing the potty dance in the drugstore aisle, you learn to make decisions quickly. In your business, there will be times when you need to absorb information and act on it immediately. When you are managing a never-ending to-do list for both your business and family, the key is to make efficient decisions, cross items off the list, and move on.

Persistence. As is the case with all businesses, yours will have some good times (your product is featured in the *New York Times*!) and some bad times (your blog is going through an approval ratings plunge). Through it all, you'll have to stay focused on your goals, rise to meet challenges, and spin every setback or obstacle into a positive learning opportunity.

Myth No. 1

BEING A STAY-AT-HOME MOM HAS LEFT ME UNPREPARED TO START A BUSINESS. When you're running your own business, every skill, talent, and experience you've ever had will be utilized in some way. If you've been managing the home finances and balancing your checkbook, those basic accounting skills will help you manage your business. Organizing your children's after-school schedules has probably given you excellent time management skills. Refereeing arguments between your children could translate into successfully mediating disagreements between your employees. You'll find that managing a family bears many similarities to handling a business.

Myth No. 2

ALL THE GOOD IDEAS HAVE ALREADY BEEN TAKEN. It's natural to get a little bug-eyed with envy from looking at work we wish we'd done ourselves. You might be pinching yourself for not being the first to have come up with the idea for binky clips. The truth of the matter is that many ideas are already out there, whether it's a reversible onesie or a whipped buttercream cupcake. Many successful products or services simply offer a fresh take on something that already exists. Innovating requires taking a look at the market's needs, current trends, or new ways (either in material or design) to reinvent an idea.

Myth No. 3

I NEED TO TURN A PROFIT AND BE ESTABLISHED WITHIN SIX MONTHS IN ORDER TO MAKE IT. Only a small handful of businesses are lucky enough to hit the jackpot in the first year. It's the rare entrepreneur who gets a large wholesale order from Target or has swells of advertisers on her blog in the first year. In the first few years, chances are you will still be chasing editors with press kits and visiting local coffeehouses to show them your artisanal sea-salt brownies. In measuring success in the early days, you should take into account the lifestyle changes you have accomplished: having a creative outlet and more opportunities to peek in on your kids during the day. While profits and company growth are certainly required targets for any business, don't beat yourself on the head by setting your expectations too high and too early.

Myth No. 4

HAVING A HOME-BASED BUSINESS WILL ALLOW ME TO SAVE ON DAY CARE AND SPEND MORE TIME WITH MY CHILDREN. The notion of working from home *and* spending time with your children may sound nice, but you'll quickly find that it's difficult to do any meaningful work when they're around. And if you try to do both at the same time, you'll realize it isn't exactly quality time for either party. Your vision of taking that call from *Lucky* magazine while your son draws peacefully in your office might be a bit unrealistic. Remember that your children did not emerge from your womb as well-behaved little citizens, ready for entry into polite society. If you have an important call or meeting scheduled, the best thing to do is to have a caregiver watch your children for that time period so that you can give the client your complete attention. Otherwise, be prepared to have that call punctuated by arm tugs ("I'm bored") and judicious, age-appropriate bribes ("Eat this M&M and be quiet"). As your business develops and grows, you'll likely have to hire a babysitter on a more regular basis to watch the kids so that you can carve out separate times for family and business.

The good thing about being self-employed is that you have the flexibility to arrange your schedule as you see fit. But beware: If you host a play date that eats up your entire afternoon, it could mean you'll be slaving away at the keyboard past midnight.

Myth No. 5

SELF-EMPLOYMENT IS ISOLATING. I'LL MISS ADULT INTERACTION. Yes, there may be times when the only adult face-to-face interaction you'll get during your workday is with the UPS driver. While you'll no longer be greeted by coworkers with "How was your weekend?" on Mondays or grabbing drinks with them after work on Fridays—you're not alone in your business. These days, since the advent of social networking media like Facebook and Twitter, running a home-based business is hardly isolating. You can engage with other creative minds and mothers throughout the day, developing a network of friends and peers. Look into online "mompreneur" groups, as well as groups for women seeking companionship in motherhood and business—they can be a wonderful place to find support.

TALK TO YOUR SPOUSE

In many ways, a new business becomes the new "baby" in the relationship. Without realizing it, the immediate needs of building your business can overpower your family's existing schedules, your personal time with your spouse, and your checkbook and savings. It's important to sit down and determine realistic expectations and shifts in routine and budgets. You will likely be investing in your business and pulling from your savings or 401(k), which can add stress especially if you are also leaving your nine-to-five job. Will your hubby be okay if your Friday date nights are replaced with order fulfillment for an indeterminate number of weeks or months? How does he feel when you blog about your little spat over kitchen cleaning? Hold a dedicated meeting with your spouse where you can sit down with a calendar and work through your scheduling conflicts, talk about plans for the family finances as you're building your business, and carve out time together. You might be taking the reins with your business, but your spouse might appreciate being able to give input regarding how his time with you and the family is budgeted.

YUMMY SPOONFULS

Organic Baby Food
Marietta, Georgia

"Eat fresh, eat local" is more than just a marketing catchphrase for Agatha Achindu; in many ways it's part of her DNA. It was just the way things were done during her childhood in Africa and Europe—food came fresh from local farmers, with no preservatives or added sugars. In 2004, having moved to Marietta, Georgia, Agatha and her husband, Georges, had their son, Jared-Zane. When it came time to start feeding solid foods to Jared-Zane, Agatha found herself turned off by the baby food offerings at the grocery store. Instead, she prepared meals for her son using vegetables from the farmers' market or meat from the butcher. Her friends (who were also mothers) would often inquire about the tasty foods she made for Jared-Zane. Soon Agatha was making large batches to share with her friends, and the demand grew so much that she started teaching workshops. Her audience quickly grew to a network of more than three hundred mothers. Propelled by her experience and motivated by a mission that "all children need to eat well," Agatha set her sights on starting Yummy Spoonfuls, a line of organic baby food, in 2006. With a product that seamlessly blends good-for-you with good taste, Yummy Spoonfuls is now carried in specialty stores, including Dean & Deluca and Whole Foods, and has received accolades, including a *Cookie* magazine award for "Best Tasting Baby Food" and the coveted Ashley Koff seal for "Most Nutritious Baby Food."

Q *Why was it important for you to make organic baby food?*

When I came to the United States in the 1990s, I was a bit paranoid about food. I didn't want to eat food that had been sitting in a can for two years. When I had a baby, I wanted to give my child the best food possible. I looked at what was called "baby food" at the supermarket and I just didn't get it. Peas are supposed to be bright green, not brownish. I think people have been programmed to think that baby food is gross—so much so that we forget that it's food. If it doesn't taste good to you, why would you want to put it in your baby's mouth?

It became clear to me—after seeing the response to my food from my coworkers and friends—that I couldn't just protect my child only. I always refer to a Maya Angelou quote, "When you know better, you do better." I realized that every child, regardless of income level, needed to eat well. Everyone should know what good food looks like and tastes like so you can expect something better. So I started making bigger batches of the food I was making for my baby so that I could share it with friends. Pretty soon, the group kept growing and I started offering free workshops to show people how to make their own baby food. And even though I have my business now, I still offer the free workshops.

 What a great philosophy! But how did you learn to cook? Did you go to school to get specialized training?

No, not at all. Growing up, we always had someone who was cooking in our home. We were always surrounded by cooking. I learned to cook when I was nine years old. And when I liked something I ate, I would just try to make it. I would just experiment with food.

 How do you make food for babies? Is there a specific process?

I make food. It is just food. Period. It just happens that both adults and babies love it. There is only one difference between what I make for adults and what I make for babies—the baby food is puréed! So if I made sweet potato pancakes for me and my husband, Jared would eat the puréed version.

Q *You didn't have any background in the food business. What were your first steps?*

I went to the Small Business Administration [SBA]. They offered free workshops on how to make business plans. The problem was, nobody knew where to send me for more help. In the South, all they knew was Gerber—no one was doing fresh baby food. I ended up going to New Mexico for a canning class, but it turned out I didn't need it. It was a lot of trial and error.

Q *How did you finance your business when you were starting out?*

I was actually a manager at a software company and I quit my job right away. There was no time to juggle both. My husband kept his job at first. Georges works on the business full-time now, handling the financial side. We actually took all our savings and cashed out our 401(k)s. We used every penny we had to start this. I was lucky that my husband believed in this. It was a lot of money to start it. In the beginning, it was really rough.

Q *When you launched, how many different flavors did you offer? And how do you go about selecting them?*

We had eighteen flavors in the beginning. We now have twenty-five. My friend is a pediatric dietetic nutritionist from Emory. And she helps me pick the recipes we should consider. We also do tasting parties where we serve dinner to adults and ask them for feedback. The foods that do well are turned into baby food.

Q *How did you get your product into the hands of consumers?*

There were already people who believed in the food I was making—a group of three hundred moms! So that was a huge base to start with, and it spread through word of mouth. In the beginning, people would order online and come by our commercial kitchen on certain days to pick up.

I did that for eight months, but I don't offer that anymore. It was too hard to deal with the amount of foot traffic coming in while also trying to make the food. Now people can still order online, but we ship it.

Q *How did stores find out about you?*

In 2009, *Cookie* magazine did a taste test for baby food and Yummy Spoonfuls won—that created an extra level of buzz and got us on everyone's radar. I started getting phone calls from news programs, including CNN. Last year, we exhibited at our first trade show, the Natural Expo East in Boston, which helped us get into stores.

Q *And how did you score Whole Foods?*

I just made an appointment with their corporate office. The woman I was meeting there tasted the baby food and screamed! It just so happened that the vice president of sales was visiting and walked by at that time. He came in and the woman told him to taste it. He asked, "Is this Italian ice?" and she said, "No, it's baby food!" So, of course, they placed an order.

Q *What tips do you have for someone who wants to launch her own line of food products?*

If you want to make a food product, don't cut corners, because cheap food products are already on the market. If you want to be successful with food, you need to make the best-quality food. And don't do it because it's a popular niche; do it because you love it It's a lot of hard work!

FINDING TIME

It's a common utterance for moms: "Where did the time go?" We all wish there were more hours in a day and even more so when we're trying to launch a business. It's important to whittle out time for your new business and creative endeavors, even if it's only two to three hours a week to start with. Finding time is not impossible but it does mean you need to pay close attention to how you spend it. Start by assessing your work habits and finding your most productive period—maybe you're sensitive to noise and find that you get more done between 6:00 A.M. and 8:00 A.M. Next, keep a journal of what you do during the week. Look for activities you can reduce to open up more time (like committing to only watching two television shows a week), places to "steal time" (like getting up 30 minutes earlier every day), or opportunities to double-up on time (like working on your laptop while waiting for your daughter to finish her guitar lesson).

CHOOSING THE RIGHT BUSINESS FOR YOU

Before you choose a business, think long and hard about this potential new line of work. Do you love to make greeting cards by hand? Are you looking to take your photography hobby to the next level? Do you enjoy writing and engaging with an audience on a daily basis? Do you have a natural sales ability? In this book, we'll give you an introduction to home-based businesses that suit creative moms: starting a product line, launching an online retail site, offering your talents as a freelancer, or pursuing a career as a blogger.

Don't choose a business simply because it's related to your previous career or it seems like it would be the biggest moneymaker. Do what you love and are passionate about—something that you can see yourself doing for the long term, not something to simply turn a buck. You will spend countless hours building your business before it makes a cent. You'll have to become your own leader. You'll have to motivate yourself to jump out of bed to work on it, even on the slow days. You'll know that you're on the right track if your business idea is taking over your life in some regard and consuming your thoughts.

FINDING A NICHE

Ask yourself, "Who do you want your customer to be?" Newbie business owners tend to answer that question by saying, "Everyone." But "everyone" is way too large and vague a target—it's massive, loosely defined, and hard to reach. Instead, you need to name your niche market, which is a group of people with similar needs and interests that can be easily identified and targeted. The good news is that you are a part of a niche market and your own best customer. Think about things you are knowledgeable about, and what needs you have that are not being met in the current marketplace. For example, mothers who wanted a way to exercise without leaving their small children in child care formed a niche market that brought about the need for things like the jogging stroller. Some of the best ideas come from personal necessity—if you're looking for it, it's likely that others in the same niche market are looking for the same thing, too.

AFFORDABLE CHILD CARE

Your business and your children need your undivided attention—and child care is the solution for that, especially when your children are not yet in school. Trust us—if you try to intermingle your two worlds, family and business, you'll get less of everything done and you'll feel more frustrated. If you want your business to succeed, you need to find chunks of time on a regular basis to accomplish work without any distraction. But before you look into child care, think about what your needs are and what you can afford. First, consider the ages of your children and what types of activities and care best suit them. Take into account the hours: the time of day and amount of time you need your children supervised per week. Do you need someone to watch the kids after school? Do you want them to be cared for at your home, or elsewhere, so you can focus strictly on work? Would you like the sitter to do light housework or driving? Depending on your needs, consider these affordable child-care options:

Family members. If your parents live nearby or you have a decent relationship with your in-laws, consider asking them to watch their grandchildren. Having someone you know and trust will reduce separation anxiety for you and your child. Another benefit is that family members will often provide this care at no cost or at a much lower price than you could find anywhere else.

Other mom business owners. Through your online or personal network, you may come across another mom with a home-based business in your area. Consider making an arrangement with her to watch your children a couple afternoons a week and you can watch hers for the same amount of time in return. It's a great no-cost solution that guarantees you'll both get a few solid kid-free hours to put your nose to the grindstone. Another solution you can work out with a like-minded entrepreneurial mom is to share both a sitter and work space—that is, hire a sitter to watch both of your kids at one home while you both work in the other home.

Tot drops. Tot drops are a drop-in day-care solution for families who need more flexibility. With this part-time, as-needed child-care option, kids can stay for a few hours. These child-care centers typically operate on a first-come, first-served basis. You'll need to make an appointment in advance to let them know you're coming and how much time your child will spend there. This may not be a reliable long-term solution, however, since there's no guarantee there will be space for your child every time you need it.

Mommy's helpers. A mommy's helper typically assists with playing and feeding the children and doing small household chores while you work from home. Teenagers and college students may be the best candidates. Mommy's helpers serve as a less-expensive solution for child care and are probably best for children who are a bit more self-sufficient. Make sure you check references and have your helper watch your children for a trial period before committing to hiring him or her.

Au pair. In exchange for room and board, a young person or college student from another country can babysit your children part-time, and maybe even help with light housekeeping.

Nanny share. Nannies are usually the most expensive form of child care, but the cost can be lessened by sharing one. If you have a friend or neighbor with kids of roughly the same age as yours, you can consider sharing the cost of a nanny. A shared nanny provides in-home care in one location to both families' children and often costs less than day care. Other benefits include the opportunity for your child to play with other children daily while minimizing exposure to a variety of illnesses. This solution works best when both families share similar child-rearing philosophies (for example, regarding television viewing and homework) and when the children get along relatively well.

STYLE ME PRETTY
Wedding Blog
Boston, Massachusetts

Tired of worrying every night about the production details of her stationery business, Abby Larson made a pivotal decision to sell it. In 2007, with her sights set on a fresh start, she started blogging about what she loved and knew best: weddings. Within a few months, her signature inspiration boards and sense of style were clicking with readers. She soon found herself with a cult-like following of brides and was taking requests from magazines such as *Martha Stewart Weddings* and *Real Simple Weddings*. The workload became so great that her husband, Tait, joined the team, providing his talents in technology and programming. The pace at which Abby and Tait have grown their blog, Style Me Pretty, has been more than impressive. In just under three years, their site has become a leading online wedding resource, with more than ten million monthly page views and nearly 500,000 monthly visitors. With two young children, Audrey and William, and a bustling business, Abby says it's not easy balancing it all, but she thanks her lucky stars that she has "the best job in the world."

When you first started, you presented something completely unique in the wedding blog world: inspiration boards based on your readers' needs. How did that come about?

When I began, there were only two well-known wedding blogs, so it was a good time to do something that no one else was doing with wedding content. At the time, most of the brides I was coming across were somewhat lost. They had all of this inspiration—stacks and stacks of wedding magazines—but had no idea how to pull it all together into one look. They would write in, telling me a little bit about their wedding, and I would come up with these very minimal, styled, inspiration boards to show them how to make a certain look come to life. I really believe that personal touch is what initially got our loyal fan following. It showed people that I had a vested interest in weddings—and in their wedding—because I created this very intimate environment. As we've grown, I stopped making them. Instead, we've built a custom inspiration board tool that allows you to access more than 500,000 images from our archives to drag and drop photos and make your own inspiration boards now.

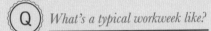

Q *What's a typical workweek like?*

The bulk of our hours are spent generating content. We post four weddings every day. But we get four to five hundred wedding submissions every week, and we manually go through and reply to every single one. The remainder of our time is spent on technology: building tools and products that make the business run smoother. For example, to help with the hundreds of weekly submissions, Tait created a custom submissions tool. Now people can load images into our galleries that later become a part of our inspiration board builder.

Q *What are some of your marketing techniques?*

From the beginning, we relied on online press and blogs to bring traffic our way. We were mentioned in major design blogs, including Design*Sponge, and that sent a huge amount of traffic to our site. For a blogger, it's really important to network with others, to generate links, and to create places for people to find you. Our goal every week is to generate a certain amount of links back to Style Me Pretty in an authentic way. We could've hired a PR person, but it costs you five to ten thousand dollars a month for great press. So we do it ourselves and it costs no money.

Q *How did you go about hiring people to help you?*

Tait and I live by the mantra that time is money. If it takes us a long time to do any one task, we outsource it. The first person I hired was 100-percent commission based, and to this day, she still is. For over a year, it was just her and me, and I only paid her what we made—so it wasn't as risky. Now, we have five salaried employees and anywhere from six to ten employees that are straight commission. We generally hire people on a trial basis—like an intern—which allows us to get to know them first. We're pretty resourceful when it comes to finding the people to work for us. Tait has recruited from a technical high school. I prefer to hire stay-at-home moms because they aren't reliant upon their income, but they really have fun with the job and they're willing to go the extra mile.

What are the dynamics of being a husband-and-wife team?

We work really well together; I don't think that a lot of people can do this. It helps that we do very different things in the business: Tait does all the technology and I do the creative. He's on the back end while I'm on the front end, more in touch with our readers. He's coming from a different perspective, so I make sure that everything he does is articulated and executed in a way that our readers will understand. Right now, we're learning to separate our day better. I know it's not ideal when we're lying in bed at night planning for tomorrow's work tasks!

How do you balance the business with being a mom? If you have any mom guilt, how do you deal with it?

As a parent, you have to be flexible every day. Every day is not going to be the same, and although you have plans in place, you have to be willing to change them without getting flustered or upset. As for guilt, it's a constant feeling. I want to stay at home and be with Audrey and William, but I also want to run my business. I need dedicated work time when I'm not taking care of the baby. If that means bringing someone in to help watch my children, I know I shouldn't feel guilty about it. To maintain a balance, my goal is to be an active mom—to be available to pick Audrey up from school, to sit down to dinner with my family, and to have two or three hours a night when computers are closed and we're just playing with the kids. As Style Me Pretty grows more, the balance becomes harder. But my children will never take a backseat to this job, ever.

STAYING FOCUSED AT HOME

When you work from home, the diversions that would sabotage your productivity surround you: The dog demands a walk, there's a pile of dishes staring at you—not to mention your daughter's Halloween costume, which needs some additional beadwork. While these things need to be done, there is an appropriate time to do them—and it's not during your work hours. Follow these guidelines to keep you focused on your business game plan.

No. 1 STAY IN YOUR WORK SPACE

Don't work in front of the television or in the kitchen where you can snack and procrastinate. One leftover pie and two peanut butter cookies later, your belly will be satisfied but you won't have checked a thing off your to-do list. Bring some healthful snacks and water with you to your office and stay in there.

No. 2 DON'T SQUEEZE IN HOUSEHOLD CHORES

It's a slippery slope from wiping the kitchen counters to reorganizing the entire pantry. Save the housework for your nonworking hours—whether at the end of the day or during the weekend. Explain to your spouse or partner that, even though you're home, you won't be able to tackle any chores.

No. 3 SET GOALS FOR EACH DAY

Create daily goals and break them down into smaller manageable bites. Aim to finish your goals by the end of the day. Also, give yourself incentives, like a five-minute facial or peaceful bath after you've put the kids to bed, to motivate you to check off everything on your to-do list.

No. 4 SCREEN CALLS AND IGNORE THE DOORBELL

If you have caller ID on your home phone, you know which calls to ignore, like solicitors. If a friend is calling, let her leave a voice message, and then listen to see what she needs. Often, when people know that you are working from home, they think that you're free to leave to grab a coffee at any time. Learn to say no and try not to entertain drop-in guests, or else they'll come back again.

No. 5 IT'S "WORK TIME" NOT "ME TIME"

Even though you're the boss now, don't even think about starting your day watching television or going to the mall—this is precious time to be doing work to support your business. Just think about the cost of your child care—that thought alone may be enough to stifle your urge to play hooky.

WHAT TO EXPECT AT DIFFERENT AGES

As your children grow, you will be making adjustments to how you do business and handle day-care needs. Here's what you can expect in the days ahead:

Newborn to Four Months

The baby sleeps a lot still, which is a good thing. Unfortunately, the saying "Sleep when your baby sleeps" doesn't apply to mom entrepreneurs. Rather, "Work while your baby sleeps" is more applicable. (Still, working at all might be an epic feat if you are completely sleep deprived and moving about like an extra in a zombie movie.) As work will largely be dictated by your child's sleep and feeding patterns, you will be working on your business in small chunks of time. Things operate slower when you have a newborn and, at this early stage, you may not be ready to hand your child to a caregiver just yet.

Five to Twelve Months

At around seven months your child will likely be slightly more mobile (crawling) so you'll need to keep a close eye on him. If you are considering getting a sitter to help you, you may want someone who can watch your baby at home so you won't miss out on the milestones like his first crawl or first word. You and your child will be a team, so get a lightweight stroller and have your diaper bag ready in case you need to go somewhere to take pictures for your blog or to pay a visit to the printer.

One to Two Years

Your child will be more mobile (taking his first step around twelve to fifteen months), sleeping less, and increasing her demands for cuddling and attention. She is going to be a little person with a personality, a temperament, and a voice. She can express what she wants with the shake of her head (yes or no) or with a limited vocabulary. When she's not understood, she might display her frustration through physical meltdowns. You will be saying "no" a lot. As your child begins to refuse to stay put, you'll find it even harder to get things done, so having child-care help becomes more imperative. This is also the age when your mom guilt may start to rear its head regularly, in response to the pleas of your children. Now that they are aware that you are "playing" with the laptop and not with them, they may not hesitate to voice their displeasure.

Three Years and Onward

Ah, school-aged children. When your kids are in school, your business falls into more of a routine and you can reliably work during certain hours. At around three years old, your child will be eligible for preschool. This is a step toward independence and children may feel a little overwhelmed at first. Give yourself time to deal with any separation anxiety that may happen when dropping them off. And even though your children may be in school, you're not off the hook—this phase of your parenthood comes with responsibilities and new involvements, such as volunteering in class and helping with school fund-raisers. With your business, you'll be spread thin—so think twice before volunteering for bigger roles in the school, like the room parent, or the president of the co-op preschool board.

When children are in school, they are exposed to more illness, especially during the winter months. Try to take fewer assignments during this time, since you may have to manage sick children or you might even get sick yourself. Holidays and vacations can be particularly challenging, since your child will be home more often. During school breaks, you may want to consider enrolling your children in day camps that can occupy them with crafts, sports, and other supervised activities while you work during the day. As your child gets older, even hosting a play date at your place may be a good option, as the kids might be able to keep themselves occupied for short periods while you get some work done.

MOM STATEMENT

Since you are a mom, you might find it helpful to also put together a "mom statement" that coexists with your business's mission statement (see Mission Statement, page 137). Think of these statements as two parts of a whole—the yin and yang—that enable you to have both a successful business and a fulfilling family life. As you would do in your mission statement, you need to describe your core values and goals as the entrepreneurial mother you hope to be. Do you endeavor to be present, active, and patient? You may even go a step further and plot out real-life scenarios that fulfill those adjectives: Will *present* mean being able to attend your daughter's tap classes *every* Thursday afternoon? Will *active* mean running for a board position at your son's co-op preschool? Next, determine what needs to be done to fulfill your goals. If *patient* means having extra time to sit down and help your eight-year-old with his homework, will this mean ending your workday at three o'clock or finding a part-time employee to take customer service calls in the afternoon? View your mom statement as a guide, reminding you to factor your family into your business decisions.

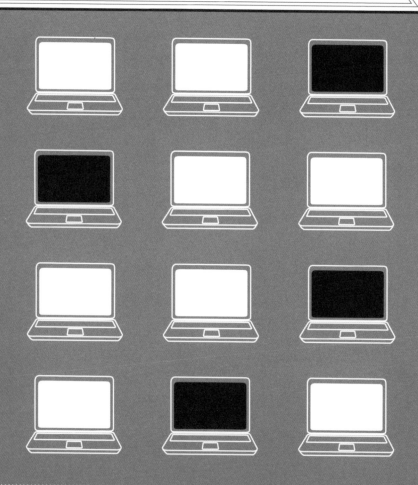

The Internet offers an **AUDIENCE OF LITERALLY MILLIONS** of people who are hungry for inspiration, information, and entertainment. And it's the stay-at-home mom with mad craft skills or the self-professed baking geek, not media icons, who satiate the appetite of these masses. They do this through blogging. At its most basic definition, a blog is basically a Web site that can be easily and instantly updated. In the olden days—like 2005—blogs used to be simple personal scrapbooks and diaries more than anything else. These days, they're part of a **BUSTLING ONLINE COMMUNITY**, and they can serve as outposts where people stop to get their fill of the news or culture they crave. They're also a **GROWING INDUSTRY**; bloggers can make anything from simple bake-sale money to **SIX-FIGURE SALARIES**. This chapter will give you the basics on this easy, even addictive, creative medium, complete with tips on eventually turning it into a **MONEY-EARNING CAREER**. With the right commitment and focus, you'll soon be pecking away at the keyboard, finding an audience, and learning why blogging is such a cultural force.

WHAT IS A BLOG?

The word *blog* is actually short for *Web log*—you can think of it as an online diary, focused on a theme or subject, with entries appearing in reverse chronological order. It's a dynamic Web site that grows with every entry, or "post," you make. As you add new posts, the older ones roll off the page and become "archives," which can be organized into categories that you define. And your readers can expand on your posts by writing comments, which give their reactions to your content. The best way to understand a blog is to actually familiarize yourself with some. It's really hard to surf the Internet without running into one, so simply do a search for "blog + [topic]"—the topic being whatever you choose, whether craft, film, weddings, humor, or news. As you get to know some of the blogs that are out there, take notes on what you like or don't like, drop comments in a few, or exchange tweets with some bloggers—once you start to engage with them, you'll begin to comprehend the allure and get a taste of what it means to be a part of this community.

THE LIFE OF A BLOGGER

It can feel enterprising and magical, and at times downright unbelievable, that a business can be created around talking about your interests. You might wonder, "If I start a blog, will people want to read what I have to say?" The answer is yes! But you'll have to be keenly aware of your environment in order to capture fodder for your blog, stick to a ritualistic schedule to create posts, and participate in social networking. It also means managing two lives: the online one and the offline one.

While all this may sound fairly easy, you might wonder, "Will I be able to earn a living from blogging?" The answer is yes, but it usually doesn't come overnight. Unless you have already achieved a level of celebrity and come with an instant readership, your blog will not start off as a business, but it will have the potential to evolve into one. It's a low-risk, low-investment venture that can only pay off with a high level of commitment and patience. So when you start your blog, our first piece of advice is to not think at all about sponsors, ads, or statistics yet. Quell those swirling stories in your head about achieving blogger stardom or becoming one of those mom bloggers who receive a free supply of diapers from a sponsor. Long before you even get to that, you'll have to find your niche and voice.

FINDING YOUR VOICE

Blogs live within an infinite universe, dubbed the *blogosphere*. Cat's blog Mom Inc Daily (originally Designing Moms) was created from a personal desire to unite design-savvy moms and readers. It was intentionally designed to be "anti-baby" (in a good way) so that moms could feel that

 Your blog will ideally be about things you are so genuinely passionate about that you wouldn't mind talking every day about them.

they had a creative and professional sanctuary of their own. Your blog will ideally be about things you are so genuinely passionate about that you wouldn't mind talking every day about them—whether it be travel, crafts, or simply you! Go with your instincts: Write about what you love and what rings true to you. After all, you are going to be spending hours, months, and possibly years expressing yourself on your blog. Don't worry about nailing your voice down right off the bat. Many bloggers attest to cringing a little over their writing in earlier posts—and that's normal. Your writing, personality, and style will evolve over time as your blog grows.

YOUR BLOG'S PERSONA

There are the bloggers whose entries sing like a chorus of angels descending upon your laptop screen, others have attitudes so wry and menacing with wit that you'll laugh to tears, and still others offer well-designed image layouts that speak volumes. It is no mystery why these bloggers have succeeded: They have tapped into themselves and developed a persona for their blog.

It's up to you to decide your blog's tone and philosophy. You can be hyper-personal and candid (revealing your innermost thoughts), personal and professional (keeping it on the surface), or anything in between. Just be sure it's an authentic human voice that you can summon at any time. If your demeanor is forced, you might develop "blogger's block" or come to resent having to write your entries.

It's important to note that your online and offline personas don't have to be identical twins. You'll find that some bloggers are completely shy individuals, while their busy little fingers are anything but. Online, they are much more extroverted than their real-life selves, with an uncanny ability to network and connect with other bloggers and artists.

However you mold your online self, remember that, when it comes to blog writing, too much of a good thing can lead to the impression that you are rambling, or perhaps overbearing. To avoid this, edit your writing and keep it concise.

WHAT TO POST

Posts can range from a single link paired with an image you found online and a brief caption to thoughtfully produced original content complete with styled images, or even a lengthy essay—really, anything goes. In general, there are five main types of blog content that creatives employ: link filter ("I found this online and here's the link to find it"), diary ("I

experienced this"), review ("Here's my opinion of this product or experience"), tutorial ("I made this, and here's how you can"), and talent
showcase ("I'm a skilled creative and this is my latest work").

Link Filter

Women (moms in particular) possess truffle-scout-like skills for finding
the best way to boil wool or the latest trendy kid sunglasses. Many of the
posts you'll find on lifestyle blogs (covering home décor, design, fashion,
food, and healthy living) are link filters. Oftentimes, the visuals on these
blogs do the "talking," featuring products in independent shops or works
by designers, artists, or chefs. Readers appreciate seeing the adeptness
of a blogger's scouting skills—not only does this clue them in to her style
and aesthetic but it also helps to emphasize the blogger's expertise on
the subject. If you mention your favorite cupcake shop, food photographer, or even the little houndstooth barrette holding your receipts,
always link these back to their sources. If the source is another blog or
Web site, make sure to give credit to the originator (for example, caption
your image with "houndstooth barrette via www.MomIncDaily.com").

Diary

Diary posts are personal in nature. They can be classified as "journey
blogs," taking readers along on your adventures—be it geographical,
cultural, or spiritual. You can chronicle your family's cross-country sum-
mer trek in a vintage Airstream or simply chat about the funny thing that
happened on the way to the grocery store. If you plan to include slices
of your day-to-day life, whether it's a shot of you and your hubby at the
flea market or a story about your daughter's first ballet performance,
you should discuss it with your spouse. While you may have no problem
showing pictures of yourself or venting about how many white hairs you
got as a result of creating that tutu, your partner might disagree and have
concerns about privacy. Your teenage son may not want the details of his
life put on display either. Ask family members to write down a list of topics that are okay and that are off limits. You can also creatively crop them
out of photos and give them pseudonyms when mentioning them on your
blog, if you think this would solve the problem.

Review

A company or a PR firm may send you a book or product to review on your blog. In a review, it's important to develop an overall opinion and clear message, while touching on both good and bad aspects about the product. Reviews aren't limited to objects sent to you either, you can do them on your own as well. For example, along with your personal story about your family's road trip, you can include a travel review with listings for budget hotels and kid-friendly restaurants. Perhaps you have a blog about your love for biking and you can include a roundup and information about the best handlebars out there. The best thing about a review is that when it's comprehensive, it tends to be bookmarked and shared.

Tutorial

If you're doing a tutorial blog, you might share daily recipes on how to cook fast, organic family meals or provide DIY instructions for things like a tote bag. The key to presenting effective tutorials is to offer compelling visuals paired with concise how-to instructions. Be ready to give blow-by-blow details on what materials to gather, how much fabric to measure, and all the nitty-gritty tips on how to repurpose a leather belt to make your tote bag's handle, for example. However, tutorials can become lengthy (and burdensome on your available time), so you may want to focus on posting projects that will offer more instant gratification, such as crafts that can be completed in ten steps or fewer, and post longer projects less often.

Talent Showcase

If you're a budding musician or illustrator, a blog can be a great way to share your talent with the world on a frequent basis. You'd be surprised: A post with your lastest humor illustration or your home-made music video featuring your latest song could make the rounds in the blogosphere. Plus, you never know who's looking at your blog—they may be inspired by your work or could hire you for a project.

ENJOYING THE SMALL THINGS

Personal Blog
Naples, Florida

A new baby, a photo, and blog post changed the course of Kelle Hampton's family life forever. Kelle, a self-taught Florida photographer and former fifth-grade teacher, first began a blog called Enjoying the Small Things (www.kellehampton.com) chronicling the life of her firstborn, Lainey, when she was seven months old. Two and a half years later, Kelle and her husband, Brett, welcomed their second daughter, Nella. But Nella's story was different—she was born with Down syndrome, something Kelle knew the instant the nurse placed her daughter into her arms. Raw, beautiful, and tragic emotions poured from Kelle into the blog post of Nella's birth story. With that, there were photographs from the birth; one in particular was a haunting photo of friends toasting with "Welcome Nella" champagne flutes in the hospital room, with a bewildered Kelle looking on from the background. The honesty of her writing, in both the poetic force of her words and photography, resonated with readers worldwide. Within days of the post, it went viral. Thousands wrote in to leave a comment. Since then, her posts continue to garner hundreds of responses from adoring readers, netting more than 1,200,000 unique visitors. As a result, Kelle's story has made its way into print—in a memoir titled *Bloom*.

Q

Tell us about Nella and how blogging helped you through this experience in your life.

The moment that she was placed in my arms, the planet cracked. I was just at the bottom, and I didn't know what I was going to do. My sister flew in the second day, and I remember telling her, "This is big." I remember telling my husband, too, that I absolutely believed this happened for a reason, and I believed that we were supposed to do something with it. Writing has always been my outlet—no matter how bad I'm feeling, if I write, I feel better. And, I knew by day three or four in the hospital—as deep, raw, and awful as I was feeling, I had to write about it. The first night I came back, I wrote the post. I brought Nell in the room with me, shut the door, and told my family and friends, "I'm gone for the night." I wrote for hours. It was almost like it was an out-of-body experience. Within a week, the post had gone viral. Those first weeks were awful—I would lie in bed in the middle of the night nursing Nella, and I would cry. I remember, I would look at my phone and there would be three hundred new comments [on the blog post]. I didn't even know these people, but it was so comforting to know that there was just this huge support network. It was a lifeline to me for probably five months when I wrote everything I thought, every bad feeling—I was having therapy with the world basically.

 What are some of the challenges you have faced with managing and growing your blog?

When you have a wider audience of people reading, there can be intense reactions to what you write. There was a post I wrote on Down syndrome that was meant to be positive; I used a metaphor of a hypothetical friend who contentedly has two boys, even though she always wanted a girl, to relate to my optimism in having Lainey and Nella. There were people who were angry because I was likening a chromosomal disorder to gender disappointment. It's still on the Internet. I've never removed it because it's a part of who I was and my journey at that point. At the same time, people have been really great supporters; there were over five hundred comments and people debating with passion. I have to constantly remind myself not to sell out, to be true to who I am, and to not be afraid to put myself out there.

 Where does the inspiration come from for the content and photography in your posts?

Very seldom do I have a post in mind. Usually, we live our life, and I will do three posts a week. I'll take pictures of whatever we happen to be doing at the moment. To get twenty pictures, I can sometimes get them in ten minutes, if we're out doing a tea party in the yard. Even if I didn't have the blog, it's very normal for me to just take pictures as we go about our life. If I don't know what I'm going to write, I have a couple regulars—I do an "enjoying the small things" post every once in a while that's basically about my favorite things. It might be about the hot cocoa I had this morning or the look on Lainey's face.

For photos, I make use of editing software such as Adobe's Lightroom where you can work with halfway decent pictures and make them beautiful. There's the argument whether being a true photographer means you shouldn't have to edit, but I believe there are different rules for photography. I learned by looking at things that inspired me, whether it was an Anthropologie catalog or the work of other photographers that I respected. I just played with my camera, and I found out what worked for me.

 How do you find balance in your day?

My husband's able to be home a lot more and so he helps out a lot. We have very flexible schedules where he'll go do his thing, come back, and say, "When do you need to write tonight?" I prioritize—it's the most important thing. My house being clean is not important to me. It's not at the top of my list, so I'll let that go until it gets to a place where I'm saying, "I can't think because of the clutter." During the day we may play "Junk Drawer"—we take everything out of it and make something. We do backyard picnics where we'll just drag a quilt into the woods behind our home.

My family and my kids come first. If I feel overwhelmed and I can't compartmentalize it, I'll call my girlfriends and say, "Help me, let's go out tonight." It's an ebb and flow—there are times when everything is just going great, and it's so smooth. And then there are other times when I feel completely overwhelmed and I just want to shut everything off. Everybody goes through that, no matter what job you have. I have two mantras: "I am capable," whenever I feel like I can't, and the other is William Shakespeare's "To thine ownself be true." This is my life, my art, and I can't let others affect me too much. Anyone in any creative field knows you have to balance being who you are while standing your ground and making people happy.

Some established or tech-savvy bloggers do everything from scratch, including self-hosting the blog and doing precision coding to set how posts and columns will appear. But don't despair—the majority of bloggers rely on customizable templates or "themes" available on blog hosting sites such as Blogger, Wordpress, and Square Space. Templates contain layouts that are already designed and coded (saving you the work) but also allow you to personalize and tweak the look depending on your needs. Whether you choose to use a template or build from scratch, here are elements common to all blogs that you'll need to familiarize yourself with.

Banner

Think of the landing page of your blog as the face that greets your reader. The area at the top of your blog will contain your blog's name—the default is usually a text version, but many bloggers opt to display a banner, or a graphic representation of the blog's name and persona. This is prime real estate, as your readers will see this first. It will give a sense of what your blog is all about, so it's important to personalize it with an interesting font along with graphics or a customized logo. If you don't have a design background, it is probably wise to invest some money and have a graphic designer create a logo and banner for you.

About

Readers love feeling connected to a blog author—they want to know more about you and your baking prowess, for example. Your "about" page should include your photo and a few details highlighting your personality. If you have a side column with an "about" feature, keep that bio to a sentence and a photo. "I am Amanda, purveyor of all things sweet and buttery in the kitchen" can give just enough of a hint regarding what readers can expect from your blog.

Categories

Readers appreciate being able to land on your blog and easily navigate it to access the information they need. To that end, categories are used to help you organize your posts instead of simply listing them chronologically on the landing page. For example, your blog on children's parties might contain categories for boys, girls, and themed birthday parties.

Comments

Comments from readers—if you allow them—will appear below each post. Readers often see comments as an extension of the post itself—a space to share their enthusiasm, add interesting tidbits to the topic, or rebut your content. You can remove, edit, or even turn off commentary on certain posts as necessary (see Managing Comments, page 47). It's an opportunity for dialogue and interaction with readers. This space is also enticing for spammers, so you want to preapprove comments or use widgets such as Akismet to filter out the spam.

Permalink

Every blog post has a "permalink"—short for *permanent link*—or its own special URL that directly links to the post. It's helpful for finding posts that have fallen into archives.

RSS Feed

Someone who likes the content on your blog can subscribe to your RSS feed (also known as Really Simple Syndication). When they subscribe to your feed, all of your blog posts will appear in a centralized place they've chosen known as a *feed reader*. Feeds allow readers to automatically get updated content from all of their favorite blogs and sites in one place. The most common and easiest way to access feeds is through a Web browser (feeds will appear as a bookmark). If you are using a blogging service or template, they'll provide the code to include on your blog so that your readers can subscribe; this will help to ensure repeat visitors and increase exposure to your content.

Blog Roll

A blog roll allows you to list the blogs you frequent and can be a wonderful way to connect with and support your online community. If you have an extensive list, consider dividing them into categories, like textile artists and multimedia artists, so that readers are not overwhelmed.

Trackback

Sometimes readers are so inspired by your blog post that they don't just place a comment on your site—they create a whole new post about the topic on their blog. When they link their commentary to your post's perma-link it's called a *trackback*.

Widgets

A widget is a compact coded program that enables you to include additional features like your Twitter feed or a shopping dictionary—to enhance your blog. Select only those that are pertinent to your blog. While a calendar widget might be a nice feature to offer readers, does it enhance your blog's experience or does it just add noise to your blog page? Consider widgets like You Might Like, which suggests previous posts that are similar in theme to the main post. (You've probably spotted this widget on many blogs, just below their posts.) It encourages readers to stay longer and continue clicking through your blog. Remember also that the more widgets you embed in your blog, the longer it may take to load. You'll typically find widgets and descriptions of their functionality among the customizing tools offered by your blogging service. (Note that Blogger calls them "Gadgets.")

ORIGINAL CONTENT

With millions of blogs in existence, you might ask yourself, "How can I provide readers with new content or a different experience?" Indeed, producing original content is one of the biggest challenges for bloggers looking to grow their site. It is also the key to their blogs' success.

 Sharing aspects of your personal life experiences will not only make the post unique to you, it will also help you to connect with readers in a more intimate way.

But what does it mean to make unique content? For one, it does not mean generating a ground-breaking idea or topic in every single post—that would be exhausting or would make every blog post a huge production. It does mean that you should approach every topic, even though it may seem passé in the blogosphere, with your unique voice and outlook. Sharing aspects of your personal life experiences will not only make the post unique to you, it will also help you to connect with readers in a more intimate way. In addition, including illustrations that you drew, photographs you took with your camera, or photo montage layouts you designed will also elevate the post's uniqueness.

When it comes to producing original content, we're often our worst enemies. Forcing yourself to put together a post under pressure ("I've got to get a post up in 15 minutes!") will lead to trite coverage of a rehashed topic. So spend time brainstorming for ideas and planning posts in advance. It also helps to cull ideas for posts by visiting places or reading publications other than blogs.

POSTING FREQUENCY

Without a doubt, you should update your blog as often as possible. Most well-known blogs post at least once a day (Monday through Friday), if not several times a day. Beginning bloggers should commit to at least three posts a week. The key is to post regularly—the more you update, the more content you will have for search engines to scan. You should also keep in mind the attention span of your online audience—with so much digital content to consume every day, many of your readers will quickly jump from blog to blog. Readers may also be looking at your blog on a handheld device and have only a small window (literally) through which to absorb information. So don't demand too much of their time with lengthy posts every day. Set a tempo that features easily digested posts, punctuated by heavier ones sporadically.

POSTING IMAGES

An image can do wonders for a post on almost any creative blog—because just talking about your handmade knit leggings or a five-tier cupcake tower you've just discovered isn't the same as showing it with a picture. When posting images, try to stick to a preset width for each image, to maintain a consistent look. You can further enhance the visual presentation by taking the time to crop, touch up, or arrange your images into an inspiration board–type layout. You can achieve this using programs such as Photoshop, Illustrator, and even PowerPoint (if you don't have access to design software). When reposting images found on other blogs or sites be sure to ask permission first, give credit, and always link the image back to the photographer or company you are featuring.

MANAGING COMMENTS

The biggest difference between blog superstars and celebrities like, say, Madonna, is that bloggers try their best to be available and accessible. They know that part of their job is to connect with readers. So respond to your readers' comments and provide a direct e-mail address for them to reach you. Even the most popular bloggers attest to reading each and every single one of the e-mail messages they receive, even if it means having to sort through hundreds of inquiries a day!

However, despite your best intentions, not every connection with your reader will be a positive one. The moment you put your thoughts, opinions, and interests onto the Internet, these can be subject to a variety of

 [T]here's a lot you can gain from a negative response.

feedback—good, bad, and plain ugly. Even though you may get used to receiving accolades from your adoring readers, there's a lot you can gain from a negative response. First, try not to take it personally and don't delete the comment immediately, although you may be tempted to pretend it never happened. If you do, you might face even more retaliation and readers might take offense. Assess the comment—is it a justified opinion, or is it mean spirited? Then address the comment directly and optimistically, and let the reader know you appreciate the difference in your opinions. If the person is attacking an artist whose work you posted, you can even defend the artist's work, if you feel it's necessary, for example. If there is a mistake on your end that someone is pointing out, take it on the chin and own up to it. An apology goes a long way. On the other hand, you should probably delete comments that are threatening, violent, or personal attacks. Ultimately, remember that it's your blog— you want your readers to feel safe when making comments, so you should moderate it as you see fit in order to keep that environment comfortable.

DESIGN MOM

Lifestyle and Design Blog
Denver, Colorado

Gabrielle Blair's decision to study graphic design in college was a calculated one: She wanted a career with the most flexibility, so she could realize her life plan to become a mother. She and her college boyfriend, Ben, knew they wanted to get married and have a big family. Indeed, the plan worked swimmingly. By 2001, the couple lived in New York along with their three children—and Gabrielle was able to help support the family with both her daily presence at home and her freelance design income. In 2006, just after baby number five was born, she began looking for a new creative outlet and a means for attracting new clients. Inspired by blogs she had been frequenting, Gabrielle started her own called Design Mom, where she shared her musings on motherhood and design. Within six months of launching her blog, she found herself with a regular readership and quickly realized that her means to attract business could actually become the business itself. Now living in Denver, Colorado, with her husband and six children (Ralph, Maude, Olive, Oscar, Betty, and June), Gabrielle is a full-time blogger. She smiles at the fact that it's the most flexible career she never planned for—reflecting the truism that the best discoveries are those that are accidental.

 What led you to start Design Mom?

I had been reading personal essay–type blogs like Everyday I Write the Book [Kasm.blogspot.com] and Mom 101 [www.mom-101.com]. Initially, I wanted to do something like that, but the problem was I was not a writer. It was not part of my skill set. Then my sister, Jordan, started sending me links to design blogs like Oh Joy. In some cases, posts were just an image and a couple of sentences. It was mostly about visual inspiration. A light clicked on and I thought, "I can do that!" It occurred to me that I could do a blog from the perspective of a mother who was also a designer. There I was, thirty-five years old in New York with five children. Most of my peers were just having their first child. So I was in a unique position to be able to give real advice to fellow mothers in terms of good gear, children's shoes, adorable party favors, and decorating—all through the lens of design.

You share bits of your personal life, including your children, on your blog. Was that a hard decision to make?

I think it's smart to base this decision on the type of content you write. If you're producing deeply personal essays about your family relationships, privacy issues definitely need to be weighed. But when I write about my family and children, it's typically showing off a project they're working on or a craft they made. My kids love the attention and enjoy the positive feedback from my readers. My oldest is now a teenager and maybe things will change. But for now, he still loves it when I mention him on Design Mom.

In 2010, Design Mom was selected as one of Time *magazine's "50 Best Websites." Without a doubt, blogging has been an amazing experience for you. How has blogging enriched your life as a mother?*

It's huge! Blogging has transformed motherhood. I've been a mom much longer than I've been a blogger, and one of the biggest things I remember in those pre-blog times was going through entire days without speaking to any other adults. It can be isolating being at home with a young baby, and it's hard if you're not being creatively challenged. When I had a newborn, there were days when I was barely functioning—even something as mundane as taking a shower was an accomplishment. Later, there would be rare and amazing days when we'd make it through twenty-four hours without any tantrums. Hooray! But there was no real way I could share these experiences and get recognition for these little achievements. With blogging, mothers now have access to validation, recognition, and support in very real ways—this underscores that what you're doing as a mother is legitimate and important.

Q *What advice do you have for someone who wants to start her own blog?*

Blogging is still in its infancy. I think it's important for people to remember that it's still a very new industry—which means it's also a bit of a Wild West playground where people are experimenting constantly. So I'd recommend jumping in, getting started, and learning as you go. When I started in 2006, I remember thinking, "I missed the chance, there are too many bloggers already." But of course, I was wrong. There's always room for something new and fresh.

Once you've jumped in, if growing your audience is important to you, you should produce quality content, regularly and often. Determine a posting schedule and keep to it. It's also important to remember that this is a *community* in every sense of the word. So don't just promote yourself, promote other people in the blogging community, too. Joanna Goddard was particularly good at this. She grew her blog readership quickly by being generous with her links to other bloggers. You have to connect to the community: Make a blog roll, answer fan mail, contribute content for other blogs, participate in activities, leave comments all over the place, and, whenever possible, respond to comments!

Q *How do you suggest people go about getting advertisers and sponsors?*

In my experience, I'd say not to worry about it until you have some traffic. You're pretty impotent until you have numbers to leverage. When you do have some numbers, go for it! Think of companies that would be a good fit and offer them deals or trades—like a blog mention in exchange for products or a how-to post featuring items from the sponsor. Come up with a price list for your services and spread the word to sponsors you'd like to work with. If the prices are too high, you won't get any takers and you can adjust them. Start with small companies that can provide the opportunity to connect directly with the owner/decision maker, then grow your sponsor list from there.

DRIVING BLOG TRAFFIC

When your blog has found its footing—shiny new banner and posts queued and all—it's time to take a look at building and maintaining your blog traffic. These days, it's not just about relaying your message solely through your blog but also about diversifying the ways in which you communicate with your audience. The first and easiest step is to actively participate in other social media platforms like Facebook, Twitter, MySpace, or LinkedIn. Doing this not only builds traffic but can also broaden your audience, allowing you to connect with new communities. (See Nice to Meet Your Avatar, page 166, for more detailed information.)

Next, you'll need to focus on search engine optimization (SEO). It sounds more complicated than it is, and thoughts of bots, crawlers, and engines scouring the Internet have been known to throw many a blogger for a loop. The goal of SEO is simple: getting your blog to show up at the top of search engine results. Thankfully, taking steps to maximize your presence in the blogosphere only requires you to add a few easy steps to your everyday blogging routine:

→ When creating post titles, use popular keywords that engines will prioritize. For example, search engines will rank the keywords "baby onesie" higher than "cotton two-piece baby pajamas." If you want to find the best words possible, utilize the Google Keyword Tool (which is free, to boot) as well as any paid keyword tools such as Wordtracker that go beyond what the Google database offers. You can also use these keywords in the body of your post. However, be careful not to crowd it with too many keywords, as search engines will consider this "keyword stuffing" and relegate your post to spam.

→ When you post images, always label, or "tag," your images with a good description or a strong keyword, to increase the likelihood that it will pop up in a Google image search.

→ Be generous with your links and link to higher-ranked sites when applicable.

→ If you post about a company or artist, use the name in the post instead of simply leaving it up to the reader to find out in a "click here" link.

INCOME AND EARNING STRATEGIES

Five hundred visits a day . . . one thousand visits a day . . . five thousand visits a day! If you see your readership growing and you're grooving to a manageable posting schedule, it's probably a good time to look at how you can generate income through your blog.

Ad Sponsors

You've probably spotted ads of all flavors on most of your favorite blogs, so it's no mystery how bloggers generate a portion, if not all, of their income. But who should be a sponsor on your site? Start by taking a look at companies and designers that speak to your niche. Is there a local shop that you frequent for all of your arts and crafts supplies—maybe for a new collage project that you'll post about? Wouldn't your readers want to know about that shop as well? Your blog could be a great place to host an ad for that shop. Reach out to them and let them know that you'd love to help increase their online presence.

Be ready to share your traffic data, because companies will want to know what they're getting for their ad dollars. The number of unique visitors and visits per day and per month will serve as the baseline data that you'll need to provide in your "media kit." This can be a portable document format (PDF) you e-mail to companies or have them download from your site. In addition to site statistics, your media kit should also include a rundown of your site's history, focus, and demographics. (Demographics can be collected through a survey given to your readers.) Additionally, it should contain information on the size, pricing, and placement of ads and if contracts are arranged on a CPM (cost per thousand impressions), monthly, or yearly basis.

It might take a period of trial and error before you get a sense of what pricing schedule clicks with sponsors. You might start off by charging $100 per month for a 125-by-125 pixel ad on your site and gradually work up to $400 per two weeks for the same size ad once your blog's readership takes off. Take a look at blogs or talk to your blog peers with similar content and readership numbers to see what their ad rates are. Be realistic and creative in your pricing—to get some ad interest going, you can even offer free placement for one or two months to your first sponsors. You should also be prepared to work with any potential advertisers to find a rate that makes sense for both of you; they may already be advertising elsewhere and will want a competitive rate from you.

As in traditional media, ad placement matters and affects pricing. Here's where it can get a little tricky. At the heart of it, you started blogging because you had a passion for travel or needed an outlet for self-expression—and you wanted to share this with the world (or, at least, the World Wide Web). You carved out this space for you, not because you wanted to lay the groundwork for an advertising income stream. For that reason, you should be conscientious about where you place ads on

 Be ready to share your traffic data, because companies will want to know what they're getting for their ad dollars.

your site and the sponsors you associate with. A common area for ad real estate is on the sides, or the "rails," of a blog page, but you can also opt to host leaderboard ("banner") ads placed prominently at the top of the pages or posts. As you can imagine, these generate the most traffic for your sponsor (and the most ad revenue for you), but they can also be distracting to your readers and a diversion from the content on your site. You may need to assess whether a giant, blinking laundry detergent ad is worth the aesthetic compromise.

Sponsored Posts

In addition to hosting ads, companies may approach you to post a review of their product or service and even compensate you for your efforts. When discussing compensation, take into consideration when the advertiser would like you to post (during a prime shopping season, like just before Black Monday, for example) and whether they are looking for more than one post installment. In exchange for sponsorship, they may also offer you free merchandise or services. Remember that transparency is key when posting "advertorials" or posts with product placement. And it's not just our suggestion—it's a rule dictated by the government. The Federal Trade Commission requires that bloggers, like journalists, disclose any connections to advertisers. In general, you should aim to post with integrity; that is, don't sell your readers on a product or service that you wouldn't want for yourself. You can choose to make the promotional connection known by saying so in the title, the text, or by crediting the sponsor at the end of your post ("Promotional consideration paid for by . . . "). Choose an option that works with your style and feels comfortable.

Ad Networks

When your blog has amassed a sizeable, regular readership, you have the option of potentially connecting with big-name advertisers (think The Gap or Target) through ad networks. Ad networks aggregate available ad space from a variety of online publishers (including Web sites and blogs) and match them with the needs of advertisers. Among niche bloggers, acceptance into ad networks like Federated, BlogHer, and Glam are coveted. However, they are selective about the blogs in their network (often requiring a minimum of 100,000 page views per month for consideration) so that they can offer the best ad placements to the high-quality brands they work with. On the other hand, a network like BlogAds has less stringent requirements, and Google AdSense allows anyone to sign up. Depending on your reach and which ad networks you decide to work with, you can earn anywhere from a few hundred dollars to well into the thousands per month.

While this may sound like easy money in the bank—you need to think carefully before signing up. Here are some concerns you should address before you join:

»→ Who are some of the advertisers in their network?

»→ What will the ads look like and will they fit your brand?

»→ Will you be able to accept or reject any advertisers or advertisements?

»→ Will you be allowed to sell ads directly through your site? And will you be able to set the prices for these ads?

»→ How much commission, if any, will they get from advertisers that purchase ad space directly from your site?

»→ How often will the ad network pay out?

AFFILIATE PROGRAMS

Another small stream of income you can bring to your blog is joining affiliate programs. If you're writing a book review anyway, the link you provide for the book can actually generate income—upward of 15 percent of the book sales price for a direct purchase from the link. Contact booksellers like Amazon or publishers like ours, Chronicle Books, for more information on their affiliate or associate programs.

GIVEAWAYS

What reader doesn't want a free copy of Ina Garten's latest cookbook or a brand-new ink-jet printer? Readers can't seem to get enough of giveaways, and they are great ways to gather attention and drive traffic to your blog. If you are planning to offer one, aim to give away an item that's related to your blog's content. Also, make it substantial and worthy of all the promotional energy you will be putting behind it. When your blog has garnered enough traffic you will find companies reaching out to you and offering up their products. If you accept, it is also a growing practice to charge an ad fee for hosting the giveaway, and for good reason. Giveaways can be time consuming: They typically last about a week, you may have to write several posts leading up to each event to excite readers, and you'll probably have to use your social network to tweet and blast out announcements to encourage entries.

Qualifying for a giveaway often means readers will have to perform some sort of marketing-related action: "like" you on Facebook, join your mailing list, tweet about your giveaway, or simply place a good, old-fashioned comment on your site. In our experience, the smallest amount of hurdles you require of your reader, the better—so don't ask for a three-action combo (we've seen it) requiring them to leave a comment, tweet, and "like" you on Facebook. After their giveaway experience, they will probably retract that "like" immediately anyway. Most important, be clear about your rules or restrictions and make sure this information is stated up front and accessible. Finally, you'll have to decide how you will pick the winner. With random giveaways, you may employ the use of a third-party random number generator such as Random.org, while a giveaway asking a reader to comment on why they should win a pair of vintage button earrings will leave the judging up to you.

LEGAL CONSIDERATIONS

False comments or defamation on a blog can revoke or shut it down without warning, so watch what you say. It's okay to have opinions, but it's not okay to make accusatory statements. Avoid saying that your mailman is to blame for delaying your shipment of party hats because he was out imbibing the night before and has a drinking problem, for example. It's also not okay for someone to leave untruthful or disturbing comments on either your blog or theirs. Take steps to request to remove the post immediately or within a certain time frame. If it still remains, you may need to look into taking legal action.

THE MOM BLOGGER

You might be an "I am Mom; hear me roar!" type of blogger or one for whom motherhood is hardly mentioned at all. Either way, you are part of a vast and growing pool of moms making the most of social networking. Jory Des Jardins, a cofounder of BlogHer (the largest online community of women bloggers, with more than 25 million visitors per month), attests to the growing presence of moms in social media. In their research, BlogHer found that, of the women transitioning to blogging, more than 70 percent were moms. Being able to log in and work virtually anywhere, with little equipment, is one of the biggest perks. Blogging has also been remarkable in that it's helped to bring moms out of isolation and into a place of expression and empowerment. Moms can now access information, from nursing advice to personal accounts of adoption, at a speed and level of intimacy never known before. Jory points out that there is a "presumption that moms aren't technologically savvy, but that's hardly the case. They're blogging as part of a platform and tapping into their natural ability to connect and support one another. They just need to trust the process of the network."

offering
A SERVICE

WE ALL HAVE TALENTS inside of us, simmering in the back of our brains, waiting to come to the forefront. As a diversion from her full-time job in market research, Meg dabbled in graphic design, which led to **FREELANCE JOBS** and eventually an invitation line. Maybe you've been known as the "portrait queen" for ages now, but taking photographs of your family and friends has always been something you thoughtfully pursued as a hobby. As you step forward with the notion that you want to offer your talents as a **SERVICE-BASED BUSINESS**, it's likely an affirming yet overwhelming prospect. In this chapter, we'll help you officially cross the threshold into **MAKING YOUR TALENT YOUR LIVELIHOOD**. As we show you how easy it can be to build a portfolio, find clients, and compensate yourself properly, you'll wonder why you kept your talent under wraps for so long.

MOM, THE CREATIVE FREELANCER

Can you imagine spending your days rolling fondant or cranking out illustrations for a children's book? Indeed, a career that rests on your creative talents can be quite rewarding. This is commonly referred to as *freelancing*, or offering your creative services to clients. Freelancers typically work by contract and are paid an agreed-upon amount to perform a specified service or create a particular product for the client. With services such as floral and graphic design, there is usually a specific end product you create for your client, like table centerpieces or brochures, while with consulting you'd provide your advice, vision, and strategy.

For mothers who want a creative business with as much flexibility as possible, freelancing ranks high. The best thing is that you can say yes to the projects you want—and no to the ones that may not be a good fit. No, wait—the best thing is that you get paid as you experiment with and develop your talent. Or—the best thing is that you get immediate validation when clients love what you've produced for them. Clearly there are lots of pros with freelancing. But freelancing isn't for everyone. You need to be the type of person who lives to dream up ideas and solutions to satisfy clients' visions, which sometimes won't align with your own. Freelancing also requires you to balance your client's schedule with your own busy calendar. And until you get a steady work flow, knowing when you'll score your next client can be a bit of a crapshoot. If you're up for that challenge, then you'll savor the very best thing about creative freelancing: watching your talent grow and seeing where that trajectory takes you. You might start off as an event planner for children's birthdays—and the next thing you know you're concocting fetes for celebrities or even penning a DIY book on the subject. Over time you may find yourself a veritable creative "slashie" like us. (Meg is a writer/designer/stylist/illustrator and Cat is a writer/designer/artist.) Once you tap into your inner creative and project your talents to the world, you won't always know what your next act is going be—and that's the beauty of it.

GET THE LAY OF THE LAND

If you've been taking photographs simply as a hobby, it's likely that the professional side is unfamiliar territory. It's time to take a look at the 'hood it resides in. In the realm of photography, there are myriad service niches from wedding and events to portraiture and editorial. Look further and you'll discover a subset of photographers with specialties or stylistic preferences—like vintage- or documentary-style photography. To find your niche, start by hitting the books and the blogs. Read up on the

 It may be a bit overwhelming at first to digest all your field has to offer, so embrace your newness to it and take it one step at a time.

icons in your field, including some who are interviewed in this book, to gain insight, glean lessons, and find inspiration. Get to know the highly regarded organizations in your field—like American Institute of Graphic Arts (AIGA) or International Cake Exploration Societe (ICES)—and search for events and conferences you can attend (see Resources, page 202). These events can be places to network with potential clients, gather information and inspiration, see the variety of niches in your field, size up the competition, and connect with vendors. It may be a bit overwhelming at first to digest all your field has to offer, so embrace your newness to it and take it one step at a time. You can start with local events like a zine fest featuring comic illustrators in your region, which may be more approachable, before hobnobbing with entrenched professionals in your field at national conferences.

CREATING A PORTFOLIO

With freelancing, your portfolio is your creative "handshake"—it intro-duces your body of work through a sampling of your talent. Depending on your field and specialization, if any, the size of your initial portfolio may vary. In general, we recommend having at least eight to ten proj-ects in your portfolio. If you're a photographer, include at least twenty to thirty images. This is our recommended minimum—but you shouldn't necessarily show everything you've ever done. The only message that will send is that you lack focus. "Simplify, simplify" is not just a Henry David Thoreau quote—it also applies to creative pursuits like portfolio

 The nature of a portfolio is that it's always a work in progress.

building. Naturally, you want to put your best foot forward, so it should include work you're most proud of. Ultimately, what matters most is that when people view your portfolio they are able to recognize your talent and creativity, sense your ambition and passion, and come away with an understanding of your definitive, signature style.

If you think you have no material to put into your portfolio, get cre-ative. You can churn out projects for yourself, clients (even if they are family members), or charitable organizations with pro bono projects—all in the name of exploring your creative potential and sense of style. Create mock logos, illustrate a poster for a concert you just attended, or shoot photographs on your trip to Argentina. Quite often the best work we do is the self-initiated kind, since these projects are more personal. All this can be used to pad your portfolio.

With your portfolio, you can also steer your business toward the types of projects you want to do. Remember that people have a hard time visualizing artistic concepts and rely on samples that you can provide to inspire them—and they usually want only what they can see. So if you don't enjoy making logos, then you shouldn't include too many. If you want to focus your talents on designing information graphics, then include a wide array of samples of those. Specializing can be a good thing because it sets you up to be an expert in that area. If you have several skill sets to share, such as photography and styling, you should create a separate portfolio for each category.

Pay close attention to how to organize your work in your portfolio—you should start and end with your most impressive projects. You can also provide any behind-the-scenes sketches or brief written explanations for any projects you want to highlight in more detail. It can be a good way to show your thought process, intelligence, and skill at taking an idea from concept to end product. When you've made your selections or designed your portfolio, print your pages on high-quality paper and bind them in book format, upload the images to your Web site as a PDF that clients can flip through, or burn the pages onto a disk for a potential client. Some professionals invest hundreds, even thousands, of dollars on their portfolio. But this is not always necessary—some of the top graphic designers or photographers still show their work in simple, wire-bound albums.

If you don't have a Web site to serve as your online portfolio, now is the time to create one. Keep in mind that your Web site should highlight your portfolio in every way possible. This means clean type and navigation options that will intuitively whisk a potential client directly to the work. There should be tabs that divide the categories of your portfolio if it is extensive. A prominent "about" button should appear somewhere on the landing page and provide your bio. If you are able to secure some written referrals and client testimonials, be sure to include these, as their endorsements will underscore the quality of your work and customer service. Your Web site can also exhibit more facets of your personality and the way in which you work with clients.

The nature of a portfolio is that it's always a work in progress. It's only as current as the day you're making it. The next day, you could be making projects that are even more portfolio worthy. It's important to know that your style and talents will evolve over time and your portfolio will have to be updated periodically, at least every two to three months, to reflect that.

AMY ATLAS EVENTS
Event Planning
New York, New York

A dessert table gave Amy Atlas, mom of two sons, a "sweet turn" from her job as a lawyer to celebrated event planner and stylist. Imagine candy-filled coned topiaries, flanking glass jars filled with pastel candy canes, macaroons arranged by color and size, and an elaborate fondant cake on a vintage, one-of-a-kind pedestal, all stylishly arranged atop a table with a geometric wallpaper background to boot. This is the kind of environment that Amy creates for her clients. With a love for entertaining and desserts stemming from childhood, Amy began to notice that cakes were overshadowing other dessert possibilities at events, especially at weddings. So she began envisioning whole tablescapes filled with confectionary wonders. Naturally, she started by creating her soon-to-be-famous tablescapes for friends and family. They were an instant hit and word of her talents spread like wildfire. In 2007, after pitching her business plan to her husband, Rick, she launched her business. It wasn't long before she was receiving praise from celebrity clients and publications like *Martha Stewart Weddings*; the *New York Times*; *O, the Oprah Magazine*; and *In Style*.

 For a lawyer who never went to a design school, your tablescapes are so creative and meticulously designed. What is your creative process?

I draw inspiration from magazines and patterns that already exist because I'm not an illustrator and I can't draw my own patterns. What I am really good at is being resourceful and knowing how to put things together. I think of myself a bit like an interior decorator; I'm not making the chair—but I know where to get someone to make the chair for me and I'll know where to place it. I know where to source everything.

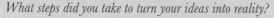

Q *What steps did you take to turn your ideas into reality?*

I started off collecting pages from magazines. I would keep an eye out for a story on a great candy manufacturer, chocolate purveyor, or baker—and the lightbulb went off that I could put all of this together. I started doing dessert tables at my own parties and then my friends and even their friends wanted one at their events. This also happened to be the time that I had a baby. In fact, all my friends were either having babies or getting married. When people walked into their parties they would say, "Whoa, I've never seen anything like this before!" Those parties helped to build my portfolio—which led to another important step I took, putting my portfolio online. When I did that, it went viral. There is a visual aspect to these tables, and people respond to that in the blog world. Since then I have started social networking, including talking to people on Twitter. I have met so many amazing designers this way. Social networking helps me be open about what I do and why. People want information—that's the age we're in. I think that the idea of being so close to the vest and keeping all the secrets is definitely more old school.

 How do you manage your business investments?

We're all about low overhead, especially in this kind of economy. I remember in the very beginning so many people were saying, "Oh, you have to get a gorgeous, sparkling office." And my husband and I would look at them like, "Are you paying for it?!" I'd rather have low overhead and pass off any savings to my client. I'm not a volume business that's mass-producing dessert tables. I work for clients who are looking for something really special. It didn't make sense for me to put too much money out there, when I wasn't even sure what the return would be yet. An investment that I did feel was important was to have a well-designed Web site. If you are in the visual world, there has to be something beautiful to showcase your work. Overall, I've been very strategic about spending. There have been many different directions where I could go (like a store, for instance), so it was always important to vet things out and see if it made sense for the brand.

How do you meet and work with your clients?

I've always been a people person so meeting clients has always been easy. I'll meet clients at restaurants or at their offices or homes. During the appointment I don't necessarily sketch; rather I show them pictures, not necessarily of dessert tables, but of different kinds of designs. I let them feel the fabric and look at different signage. I'll also show them pictures of my own work. I try to get a sense of what their aesthetic is when I show them these things. Do they like boho chic? Do they like neutral, monochromatic tones? Do they want pops of color? I just try to draw that out of them in that meeting, so it feels like their party. Most of my clients have a sense of what they want.

How do you juggle your day?

It's a constant balance. You want to go to your kid's soccer game, so you go to the soccer game but then you're looking at your BlackBerry. You can't help but feel the guilt. But at the same time, I feel like it's a better balance than having a full-time job would afford. We also have a great live-and-work setup where the studio is next door to the apartment and my boys can see me if they want to. I really do try on an everyday basis to turn myself off when I officially come home so that I can be 100 percent with my family. I make dinner with them, eat with them—that's our time, because after a long day, they have a lot of information in their heads and they need Mom. In the morning, my husband usually takes the kids to school, and I'm doing the blog post in the morning and the craziness begins all over again! My son can sum it up best . . . "Sometimes my mom does these parties and sometimes she does photo shoots and sometimes she's on TV, but she's also a lawyer." I love the fact that they can look to me and say, "My mom works." I think that's important whether it's setting the tone or serving as that role model. I think they are aware I do a lot of different things in my business.

FINDING CLIENTS

Acquiring clients means you need to make your talent and services known—otherwise, how will people know you're a whiz at stop-motion videos or that you can draw photo-realistic images? Getting your portfolio online is one step, and the other is getting your name and portfolio in front of potential clients.

Truth be told, clients are all around you, from your Pilates instructor to your husband's golf buddy. You just never know who may need your services (or who may know someone who does). Since every personal contact carries the possibility of developing into a professional relationship, don't be afraid to toot your own horn and make it known to people what you do. An "elevator pitch" isn't just for Hollywood; you should be able to explain, in a clear and engaging manner, what you do, in under a minute. (Of course, you shouldn't be promoting yourself at all times or your proselytizing will fall on deaf ears and you'll risk damaging your relationships, so choose your moments wisely.)

Put together a spreadsheet of potential clients—both attainable ones and those who may seem out of reach. If your sights are set on landing bigger clients, like publishing houses or advertising agencies, research their mastheads and Web sites to find the names and contact information of art directors or editors. But remember that it doesn't hurt to start small and get your feet wet first—which means pitching your illustrations to the local newspaper before hitting up the *New York Times*, or planning a twenty-person birthday party before attempting a three-hundred-guest retirement party. With bigger clients comes more responsibilities and higher expectations, so do it only when you are ready.

You'll be amazed at how many companies need freelancers for jobs but don't have time to find the right person. If you introduce your work, you may actually be helping them out. Put together self-promotional packages including either a postcard or a small printed sample of your portfolio to mail to everyone on your list. Most important, after about seven to ten days, follow up to arrange meetings or phone calls. As with any type of self-promotion strategy, you'll learn that it takes time—you may need to place yourself in front of a client several times before he or she bites.

One word of caution: Be careful about growing too fast and taking on too many clients. If you're not prepared, you can sink your freelance career. If you're running your company at a speed determined by your clients, not by you, you'll run yourself ragged and your ship will veer wildly out of control. Rapid growth is exciting, but excitement can quickly turn to anxiety when you realize that you can't give sufficient focused attention to all your projects within the deadlines you've agreed to.

ENHANCE YOUR SKILLS

Centuries ago, the only way to become an expert in a trade was through years-long apprenticeships following the masters. These days, while far less romantic, you can get additional training from professionals through two-day workshops and even virtually through YouTube tutorials. Staying at the top of your game requires familiarizing yourself with tools to improve your skill and efficiency, like learning how to do "actions" in Photoshop. It can also mean experimenting with new techniques, such as an old-school photography method like wet-plate collodion. As you become more entrenched in your talent, you'll find that cultivating your talent and turning it into expertise—like the craftsmen of yore—takes time.

WHAT TO CHARGE

Even though we said that you should pick a talent or field that you love so much that you'd do it for free, actually doing it for free isn't a sound business practice. So what should you charge? In freelancing, you'll have to propose an estimate to a client or your client will come to you with a budget—either way, you need to assess what your time and the project is worth.

While it may be tempting to just randomly pick an hourly rate that sounds good—it's best to know the right dollar amount to cover your business and personal expenses. The best way to figure this out is to create a budget and then break it down into hourly chunks.

YEARLY BUSINESS BUDGET

Auto	$180	Mileage for meetings with clients
Travel	$600	Flights, trains, taxis
Meals and Entertainment	$500	Meals with clients
Professional Fees	$800	Fees for your accountant or lawyer
Dues and Subscriptions	$75	
Licenses and Permits	$125	
Insurance	$800	Health and life insurance
Marketing and Promotion	$2,000	
Internet	$500	
Postage and Delivery	$200	
Telephone	$900	Cell phone or dedicated business line
Office Supplies	$400	
Starting Salary	$30,000	Enough to cover your personal expenses
Business Reinvestment	$24,000	Profit to reinvest back into the business
Total	$61,080	

The total is your goal—what you aim to earn in your first year. Take this number and divide it by your billable hours. While you may think it's pretty safe to assume that you'll be working on your business 8 hours a day in your first year (40 hours a week over 52 weeks), all of those hours aren't exactly billable—you won't be able to charge every one of those hours to clients. To figure out how many actual billable hours you'll put in, start by subtracting time: You'll probably take some time off for a vacation with your friends or family (2 weeks), you'll probably be sick or taking care of a sick child (let's assume 2 weeks), and you may be shuttling kids to after-school classes, hosting play dates, attending conferences and networking events that will cut into your work day (let's say another 2 weeks). That brings your yearly total down to 46 weeks—which, when multiplied by 40 hours, is 1,840 hours. Once you're in the thick of it, the billable percent of these hours may be 60 to 70 percent—meaning the remaining 30 to 40 percent of your work time will be spent on activities like meetings, bookkeeping, marketing, and self-initiated work. However, in the beginning you'll be ramping up business and the amount of administrative, marketing, and portfolio-building tasks will be even greater—pushing your billable hours lower, likely closer to 50 percent. Here's what that scenario might look like:

Billable hours for the first year

50% x 1,840 = 920 hours

Starting hourly rate

$61,080 ÷ 920 hours = $66.39 per hour

(you can round it to $70 per hour)

The hourly amount you reach is your baseline rate, the minimum amount you need to charge to make your freelance career a lucrative and worthwhile pursuit. If you're relatively new to your field, you may want to stick with your baseline rate for the first few months. Your hourly rate can also help you to establish base costs for a menu of services or offerings—like logos, complete identities, or Web site design. If you're providing items that use raw materials, like floral arrangements, for instance, be sure to include those costs on top of the hours.

Depending on the job and client, and as your experience grows, you may find reasons to go above your baseline rate, or you may encounter situations that dictate going below it.

How to Know When It's Time to
Increase Your Hourly Rate

➤ You checked your market and industry standards for your service, and it lists a higher hourly figure.

➤ You checked your competitors and peers with a comparable level of experience—and they're charging more.

➤ You're offering a very specialized service that doesn't have much competition.

➤ You're working with a difficult client and a higher fee could offset a potentially nightmarish experience.

➤ Your client is requesting a rush job.

➤ You have exceptionally busy seasons, like shooting family portraits right before the holidays.

How to Know When You Need to
Decrease Your Hourly Rate

➤ In the beginning, you may have to price your services competitively in order to get your foot in the door.

➤ The job is more artistically fulfilling and will be good for your portfolio, so you don't mind getting paid less.

➤ The client has a low budget for the job, but having this company on your client list is an impressive endorsement.

MEETING WITH CLIENTS

If you're working from home, you may not have a dedicated space to meet with clients—and there may be a slew of personal reasons why you wouldn't want a stranger in your home for a meeting. Your meeting spot will likely be a local coffee shop or restaurant. Scout out a mellow, well-lit venue in advance, one where you will not be constantly interrupted by loud espresso machines and rock music blasting from the speakers, you can plug in your laptop if needed, and you can lay your portfolio or spread out any paperwork on ample table space.

Within your niche, you may have clients who demand different service protocols. In photography, editorial clients and bridal clients are often like night and day. When meeting with clients, you may have to hold back your artistic inclinations for a bridal couple with specific requests. On the other hand, you may need to show your most unique and aesthetically daring work when trying to land an editorial feature. Always research your clients' backgrounds. Before your first meeting, send them an e-mail with a short list of questions about the project that will show you're engaged and have done your research—their answers may help you clue into what they are looking for.

IT'S ALL NEGOTIABLE

Even though a client comes with a set budget or a fee proposal for your services, there is often room for negotiation. Don't be so excited to get your foot in the door that you simply agree to the first set of terms and fees they suggest. If you do this, this can set a precedent for all subsequent jobs. Remember that it's in your client's best interest to secure your work at the lowest budget and with the most rights, while it's in your best interest to ask for a higher fee and retain the most rights to your work.

TIPS FOR MAKING YOUR CLIENTS HAPPY

- Listen to your clients. Make an effort to really understand them; don't just churn out a product that satisfies mainly you. Pay attention to their feedback to find a balance between injecting your aesthetic and meeting your client's needs.

- Return e-mail and calls within one or two days, especially if you don't have the benefit of being able to meet face to face on a regular basis.

- Check in regularly. Follow up on any questions or concerns they might have. Even if they seem like happy clams, shoot them an e-mail every now and then during the course of a project to let them know how things are going. Being pro-active will make them feel that you are making them a priority and are on top of the schedule and deadlines. Taking this action will help you win over their trust and loyalty.

- Beat the deadlines. Surprise your client by turning in sketches a day or two early!

- Send estimates, contracts, and invoices promptly. If you show efficiency and organization, your client will take note of your professionalism.

- A note or a gift makes people feel special. If you have extra letterpress greeting cards from a print run, for example, you can bundle them with your business card and give them to a client after a first meeting. At the end of a project, sending a lovely thank-you note to your clients will enhance their experience.

You'll have to provide an estimate to your client that details the parameters of the job, the deliverables, and your fee. Your estimate can also double as a contract. Here is a sample of what an estimate can look like:

1 Logo and contact information

2 Date

3 Client's name, address, and contact information

4 Estimate number

5 Description of the job: what the job entails, including any quantities of items

6 Timeline: milestones for the project, including when sketches, rough drafts, and the final project are due

7 Fees: total amount due for the project (itemized if necessary), with your hourly rate in case the job ends up requiring additional work outside of the description

8 Rights: what rights you will retain or transfer to the client

9 Terms: when a deposit and full payment are due as well as any cancellation fees and preferred payment methods

10 Expiration: the length of time the estimate is valid (usually thirty to ninety days), so that clients can't return in several months expecting the same fees

11 Approval: an area for the client to sign and agree to the contract

(1)

DAHLIA DRAWS
1157 B Post Street
San Francisco, California 94123
415-555-1100
dahlia@dahliadraws.com

(4)

No. 10323

ESTIMATE

(2)

DATE:
February 1, 2013

(3)

COMMISSIONED BY:
Karen Director, Crafty Site
1100 March Street
Los Angeles, CA 90025
kmoors@craftysite.com

(5)

ASSIGNMENT DESCRIPTION:
Ten (10) illustrations to be used as badges on the Web site.

(6)

DELIVERY SCHEDULE:
Sketches due by February 15, 2013. Five (5) final illustrations due by March 2, 2013, remainder by April 3, 2013

FEE PAYMENT SCHEDULE:
50% due at 1st delivery, 50% due at final delivery

(7)

ESTIMATED COST:
$1,200 (at $80/hour)

(8)

RIGHTS TRANSFERRED:
One-time electronic rights only. Any usage rights not exclusively transferred are reserved to the Illustrator. Usage beyond that granted to the Client herein shall require payment of a mutually agreed-upon additional fee subject to all terms. Any transfer of rights is conditional upon receipt of full payment.

(9)

TERMS:
Time for Payment is due within 30 days of receipt of invoice. A 1½% monthly service charge will be billed for late payment.
Cancellation: If job is stopped for any reason this % is due: After Sketches 25%, After Tight Drawing 50%, After Final 100%.

(10)

EXPIRATION:
The current estimate will be honored for 60 days.

(11)

CONSENTED AND AGREED TO:

_____
Dahlia Draws, Illustrator

_____
Karen Director, Client

_____
Date

_____
Date

interview

№ 6

SIXX DESIGN

Interior Design
New York, New York

Cortney Novogratz and her husband, Robert, are the inspiring and hip team behind Sixx Design, known for designing spectacular living spaces in Manhattan and beyond. Among the eclectic array of spaces they've designed are homes with walls that mix scrap vintage letters with goose-feathered light fixtures, and even a mini basketball court off the foyer. Without any formal training in design or architecture, the duo shadowed contractors and architects and infused what they learned with their unique sense of style and love for high and low art and antiques. And they've done all of this while growing a family: seven children to be exact (Wolfgang, twins Bellamy and Tallulah, Breaker, twins Five and Holleder, and youngest Major). Now they find themselves at the helm of numerous design projects, including private residences and hotels, not to mention being the stars of the reality show, *Home by Novogratz*, as well as authors of an interior design book, *Downtown Chic*. Cortney and Robert have successfully managed to express the credo "We live by our own rules" throughout their designs and family life.

How did you meet your husband, Robert? And how did you know that you could come together to create both a large family and amazing design?

Robert and I met at a party in the South, and we ended up moving to New York. We knew from the start that we wanted a large family; we never knew how many kids, but we both knew it would be big. And if we wanted to stay in New York City, we would have to live by our own rules. We bought an empty building and put everything that we owned into it. Everyone thought we were crazy. But we knew one day it would be beautiful and that it would be our home. We also knew having three full-time jobs (a desk job, design, and children) was not sustainable. So we decided that, no matter how financially strapped, we'd be a little more stress free if we eliminated one of those. It was scary for Robert to walk away from his job, but it was evident that this was our passion and that no matter what, if we failed, we would fail together. We could always start over.

 Neither of you has a formal design background, but you have worked extensively on major design and remodels of homes. How did you manage to find your way?

Robert and I both grew up loving architecture and design, and his parents even happened to own an antiques store. We were constantly surrounding ourselves with design, so it's not too surprising that we ended up finding careers in it. Although I've been in the city for twenty years, I remember when I first moved here, I didn't know where anything was. I had a friend in costume design and I'd ask her where to find vintage fabrics. She didn't have anything to do with designing homes but she was a great resource. An important thing to do is to always ask questions and surround yourself with people in the trade and learn from them. Ask them where they go, what their sources are, and what tricks they use. To this day, if I'm at a table with an architect, I'm always listening, because they have studied, have a degree, and are licensed. I'm often surprised that I know just as much—just learned in a different way—from all the years of paying attention and listening. You really need to open your eyes and ears to every person.

 What is your approach when working with clients who put their trust and living spaces into your hands?

Once you start answering to someone else you realize that ultimately they need to be happy. You might push a little bit to do something different, but then they are the ones who have to live there at the end of the day. I had a client in Palm Beach who was reluctant to have stripes painted on the walls of her home, so I had to take time to talk to her about it. We called it "stripe therapy." You have to allow some people to sit with things a little longer before they are comfortable with it. Another thing that Robert and I realized, too, is that when you talk about home and money with people, it brings out a lot of anxiety. We're good at helping clients feel comfortable with their decisions and investments. We'll always remind clients who are a couple: "You obviously found each other for a reason. You got married for a reason and you are creating a home for a reason. You can enjoy the process versus feeling stressful about picking out your bedroom paint color or your bathroom tiles." With clients it's important to remind them to take a step back and enjoy the transformation.

 Most people would assume that with seven kids you have an outside office space. Where do you work and what's your daily routine like?

Our work space is here. We have all of our tiles and fabrics and samples up in the corner of my bedroom. Quite literally, we have no other office, except on the job site. If we did, we would have to pay rent on that proper office. And we would also be in a separate location from our children. I may be popping in and out, but everything is underneath our roof, so I feel like I'm able to still pick my kids up from school if they have a problem. We do everything when our six older children are at school. So, come three o'clock, we try to shut down everything because at that point—forget it! There are tutors at the table and homework all over the place. Of course, we still have a contractor stopping in after hours every now and then to give us updates, but for the most part we try to have meetings before the kids are home because it's quiet and we can actually speak to the architect we're meeting with.

 What kinds of challenges do you think mom entrepreneurs face?

The biggest challenge for moms is we can't be at the top of our game and be the best mom and make every school event—we have to somehow walk a balance and choose what we can do. I think constantly about trying to get the kids to eat healthfully and do their homework, but you give them the piece of candy from time to time because you have to make certain compromises.

FINDING VENDORS

A freelancer is often like a film producer—she is responsible for putting together a team to make a successful end product. If you're a graphic designer, you'll probably need to have a stable of printers, binderies, and paper suppliers. If you're a party planner, your team will include rental facilities, party supply stores, and florists. For a photographer, it's lighting equipment rental shops, film scanners, and album wholesalers.

 School yourself on any technical terminology or trade knowledge before approaching vendors for estimates.

You need to keep a Rolodex or files so you can collect contact information for the vendors you prefer as you come across them (at trade shows or around town). Pick up any information on the range of services or products they provide as well as pricing details. Ask friends or colleagues in your field for recommendations as well. Whenever a project comes up, you can refer to your file or Rolodex with ease and contact suppliers with questions or request quotes. School yourself on any technical terminology or trade knowledge before approaching vendors for estimates. If you're going to a florist on behalf of your wedding client, you'd better have a good idea of what blossoms are in season—otherwise, you may look amateurish, resulting in higher price quotes and perhaps less cooperation from the vendor. Finding a vendor who provides good customer service and high-quality work at a competitive price is golden—they'll soon earn a permanent spot on your team.

Landing jobs takes perseverance—it's an endless process of getting your work out there, in front of potential clients and buyers. You'll likely have to update your Web site with new projects, e-mail samples of your work, and set up meetings to show your portfolio. On top of that, you have to follow up with e-mails to stay on their radar. It's a constant cycle of self-promotion and it's something you'll need to be comfortable with in order to succeed as a freelancer.

If you'd rather focus on creating work and developing your talent instead of working one-on-one and developing relationships with clients, then getting an agent may be in your future. Having an agent can do several important things for you: foremost is land you high-profile jobs and clients that would have been difficult to score on your own—like photographing an advertising campaign for Apple or creating a book cover illustration for a best-selling author. Other perks include securing higher fees for your talent, negotiating contracts on your behalf, billing and collecting payments from clients, and implementing a marketing plan. Of course, all this comes at a price: Agents take a commission from your fee, anywhere from 15 to 50 percent (with 15 to 25 percent being the most common).

Putting your career in the hands of an agent means relinquishing some of the control you have over it. You'll need to take great care in finding the right agent for you—one who has your best interests in mind and will find work that pushes your talent to the next level, not merely feed you jobs that pad his bottom line. The best way to track down an agent is to look online (agents' names are listed on Web sites of freelancers) and to get recommendations from colleagues. Remember that different agencies have varying criteria in their talent search: Some may be looking for ground-breaking new talent while others want seasoned professionals with a well-established aesthetic. Regardless, they are looking for someone with a novel style to offer rather than the talent already on their roster. When you've narrowed your dream agents, review each agency's Web site to see the submission guidelines. If an agency shows interest in you, try to set up an appointment to meet face-to-face. You'll be interacting a lot with your agent so you want to make sure this is someone you respect, trust, share a good rapport with, and can envision developing a long relationship with.

FRIEND-CLIENTS

As the saying goes, if you build it—and offer sixteen different cake flavors—they will come. And come they will, including friends and family requesting discounts and maybe even freebies. It is inevitable and possibly slightly annoying. With these friend-clients come the occasional late payments, final proofs that take forever to approve, endless minor tweaks along the way, and requests on the tightest deadlines ever. Upon giving them their deliverables, you'll probably mutter, "I'm never doing another job for a friend!" But inevitably, you'll learn that it's not so easy to say no to your best friend or mother-in-law.

Working with friends doesn't have to be a burdensome chore if you set expectations and ground rules as well as vet their readiness to work with you. Make sure you keep good written records about what end product they are getting, in case of a potential disagreement, and state pricing clearly from the beginning—especially if you've agreed to extend a discount to them. Also, if you explain how busy you are, your friends may learn to respect your time better—and remember to hire you with enough lead time next time around. If you have a feeling that working with a friend is going to be a nightmare, find a kind way to say no ("my workload is way too heavy right now") or quote a high enough fee that the cost will either be a deterrent for them or an incentive for you to deal with any "friendzilla" behavior during the process. If a relative or close friend requests a freebie, suggest turning it into a bartering deal instead—in exchange for your work on her business cards, she could watch your children for a couple afternoons.

creating
A PRODUCT

With **INSPIRATION AND PLANNING**, the homemade "thingamajig" you concocted out of recycled shirts to make an incognito nursing cover can **BECOME A PRODUCT ON THE SHELVES** of a maternity boutique. But sometimes the **DRIVE TO CREATE** doesn't come from discovering an ingenious solution to a problem—sometimes it's purely accidental. Maybe you grabbed some pom-poms, an elastic headband, and a glue gun to make a hair accessory to wear to a party—and the next thing you knew, partygoers were egging you to **PUT YOUR DESIGNS UP** on Etsy. Now, you might be wondering, "Where do I get two hundred pom-poms that won't cost me an arm and a leg? **HOW MUCH SHOULD I CHARGE** and how should they be packaged?" This chapter will demonstrate what it takes to get your product, including those of the edible variety, into the hands of the masses.

THE "PRODUCTIVE" MOM ENTREPRENEUR

Thankfully, we haven't experienced any differences in our capacity to design products before and after kids. Yes, there are now both production *and* school schedules to contend with. And, sure, we may have spotty short-term memory, but the creativity to ideate and produce a product from scratch has thankfully remained intact. Designing a product takes myriad problem-solving skills, from creative ("How do I give soap a vibrant coral hue?") to analytical ("How many clothing labels should I source and factor into initial production?"). Every product requires a succession of decisions such as drumming up a concept, researching and sourcing materials, testing and receiving feedback, and manufacturing before it reaches the final stage of being ready to go out the door.

IDEATION

It has taken us anywhere from months to design a collection of wedding invitations to just two weeks for an eco-office product. In the beginning, until you're comfortable with it, it's perfectly fine to ease into the process

 [I]t's perfectly fine to ease into the process of dreaming up your product and even nurturing it for a little while.

of dreaming up your product and even nurturing it for a little while. It's called *ideation* and your initial ideas can come in different forms—a concrete product, an abstract thought, or a rough visual. The cycle of

ideation is complete when it goes through the full process from concep-
tualization to actualization. Depending on your niche and brand for your
business (see Finding a Niche, page 22, and Establishing an Original
Brand, page 136), you can think up ideas that may be solution oriented,
like creating a device to hold a sippy cup on a stroller; symbiotic, like
bringing together knitting and ceramics; artistic, such as adorning oven
mitts with a red-hued deer appliqué; or even serendipitous, such as
accidentally spilling balsamic vinegar into your cupcake frosting. You
never know when that eureka moment will strike you, so it helps to keep
your mind open while also challenging yourself to ideate.

Unbottle Your Creativity

So much of a mom's life is focused on controlling the schedule, getting
the mouths fed, and keeping the train on track that it's easy to lose sight
of the value in veering off course every once in a while. Let yourself
daydream, experiment with baking, write stream-of-consciousness style
in your journal, chase links online to see where they take you, or put away
the laptop and go for a hike. Most important, make sure you document
your thoughts and observations. Keep a notebook, take photographs and
print them out, make an inspiration board, or use inspiration-cataloging
Web sites like FFFFOUND, Pinterest, or Evernote.

Go Trend Spotting

We like to think of trend spotting as a game—flip through magazines,
scan through blogs, and hit up some of your favorite stores and boutiques
and take note of any overarching trends you see in products, colors,
materials, motifs, or patterns. This exercise will inform you of what *not* to
do, leading you to form better ideas. When the market is starting to get
saturated with a particular trend, it's only a matter of time before mass-
market companies catch on and drive it down to homogeneity—so you'll
want to avoid catching the coattails of a trend that's on its way out.

If you haven't noticed already, the baby and kid market has exploded in the past few years. Parents are demanding more practical, personal, stylish, and organic products than ever before. Naturally, this has also become a pretty competitive niche. During your ideation process, if you want to be ahead of the curve and see what's happening in this industry, we suggest attending trade shows like ABC Kids Expo or American International Toy Fair. (See Trade Shows, page 102, for more information on how to gain access to them.)

If you're looking into creating baby accessories, you'll notice that in retail stores and on sites like Etsy there are a plethora of baby blankets, booties, burp cloths that look remarkably similar to each other, aside from their label. So how do you create a product that is unique enough to stand out in an Etsy lineup? For one, take a look at the materials you are sourcing. If you are using the same apple print fabric as the next designer for your animal plushies or screen-printing designs onto the same American Apparel onesie, consider designing your own pattern (you can print small runs at Spoonflower.com), using hard-to-find vintage fabrics, or finding a pattern maker to design a unique onesie.

If you want to create children's toys, games, school supplies, or crafting kits, think first about the age group you are catering to and how these products will be made. Since you will likely start out as a cottage industry operation, you should start with small products that can be made in a limited production space (like your garage) with basic tools and facilities—think hand-painted blocks, not teak roller-coaster toy sets.

According to the Consumer Product Safety Commission (CPSC), if a product is intended for use by someone twelve years or younger, it is considered a children's product. You will need to use high-quality materials at all times, label the product package with the intended age group of the user, and be sure your product meets the current CPSC's standards on children's products (visit CPSC.gov).

After ideation comes *prototyping*, or creating a finished sample of your product. Since your family members are the only people who have been privy to what you've made, you need to share it with others to get their feedback. Indeed, doing market research, or understanding your customer or market, is a useful way to sift your ideas into "what works" and "what doesn't work" piles, predict how well your product may do, and give you an idea of how to price your goods.

Trying to figure out whether moms will flock to buy your innovative baby side sling takes some healthy optimism that your research—however ugly or resplendent the truth might be—will ultimately refine and benefit your product. By receiving feedback from your market, you may discover new ways to make your product more user friendly, or maybe even more practical or outrageous. The buyer's perspective is invaluable. The following are different ways to tackle your research:

No. 1 GET GENERAL FEEDBACK

We think back to how invaluable it was to get some down-to-earth, honest advice from the people we trusted—even if it stung a little to hear that our camouflage pattern looked more like "indeterminate fungi." Going back to the drawing board was ultimately the wisest move. For starters, you will need to decide who will make the cut in becoming your ultimate confidante or critic. Create a list of trustworthy individuals, like family, friends, and members of mom or craft groups.

No. 2 CONSULT A SEASONED DESIGNER

You might find that designers are reluctant to reveal their secrets, but some might be willing to give you feedback on your product (provided you're not a potential competitor). Before you blindside one, try establishing a friendly relationship first.

No. 3 MAKE YOUR OWN FOCUS GROUP

Put together a focus group of people (with a range of personalities) in your market—whether that's a bunch of eight-year-old girls in your daughter's class or several of your girlfriends—present them with your product, and watch them interact with it. In order to get the most meaningful feedback, try not to overwhelm people with too many ideas or choices. Instead of presenting a dozen potential patterns that you're considering for a bedding line, cut the number of choices in half. For the purposes of discovering insights, ask them open-ended questions: "How does this glazed bowl make you feel when you hold it in your hands?" "How much would you pay for this set of candles?" You can also elicit honest responses from people by stealthily including them in your focus group. You can serve up your vegan cherry scones at a brunch, for example. If you notice that people are excited about what you've made, take it as a good sign.

No. 4 DO SOME MARKET RECONNAISSANCE

Scan blogs, retail shops, and your competitors for any products that are similar to what you want to make. Look at their price points and also at the commentary on blogs or on sites where you can see customer ratings and feedback. Use that free consumer feedback to inform your product design.

No. 5 ATTEND A RETAIL SHOW

Retail shows, like craft or street fairs, can give you a sense of how consumers are reacting and responding to products in person. If you see several silk-screened shirt booths, notice which one is attracting the most traffic: Do their shirts fit better or are they made of softer cotton? Are their owl and wolf illustrations causing a stir? Are their prices lower? Consider attending even more-targeted retail shows, such as those that attract women or mothers, for a more discriminating view of your market.

SKIP HOP
Innovative Baby and Children's Products
New York, New York

When you can't find it, make it. At least that was Ellen Diamant's thought about her diaper-bag dilemma in 2003, after the birth of her son, Spencer. Her main problem? She couldn't find one that was both fashionable to wear and functional to hang on a stroller. Initially, she didn't set out to make a dent in the baby market; she simply wanted to make some bags for herself and her friends—until her husband, Michael, convinced her otherwise. "If *you* want it, maybe there are other people who would want it, too," Michael urged her. And he was right. When they took their Duo diaper bag—hailed as the first "stroller bag"—to ENK Children's Club, a trade show in New York, the bags exploded on the scene and orders piled up. It just goes to show that two people with nothing but an enthusiasm for innovative design can go from mom-and-dad consumers to industry leaders in the baby market.

 Walk us through the product development phase of the Duo diaper bag.

We started sketching and found people in New York to make the prototype. We weren't sure what the sample would look like. We had to keep an open mind and remind ourselves that this was not just for us but would be something that other people would use and enjoy. We'd never made a bag, so we found a technical person to help us with some sketches. We found a manufacturer who could sample it, and we went through many, many samples. The first one looked like a camera bag. The second one came out looking like a pocket book. The key to this product was that it was going to be unisex—that a man could carry it, a woman could carry it, and that was a really new concept. It was a huge deal to do the first prototype. The process took us nearly a year! With our final prototype, we asked friends and local retailers for feedback. We always called retailers in advance and never popped in. Retailers, especially independent ones in the baby business, are generally really open. They'll take a look at your things. We received feedback from two New York retailers who loved it but wanted cheaper pricing. We adjusted things a little and then did ENK Children's Club in New York City—and orders took off.

How did you handle marketing and getting the word out?

I leaned on my branding experience and we actually did our own marketing. As a graphic designer, I did my own design. For our logo we wanted it to be sleek, modern, and have a very simple look. We were very particular; we designed a few different logos and took votes. I think that if you don't have a design background, it's worth every penny to recruit an outside professional designer to do it. Your branding and logo are so important. It's your face; it's how people see you. For photos, we had photographer friends help out and recruited friends to be models. Everything was done on a shoestring. But we also made sure that it looked really professional, because there's nothing worse than *not* having professional branding. You don't want to look "mom-and-pop-y," even though you are mom and pop. You really want to create the impression to your consumers that you are established, you will be able to deliver this product, and you're not making it in your basement, even though you are.

The baby and kid market is so competitive. What does it take to create something that both retailers and customers want to buy?

A lot of the people who are starting baby-product companies are moms or dads who obviously know what they want. But those items don't always translate into businesses. Sometimes the market is overwhelmed. Sometimes it exists already. If you have a concept or an idea, it's important that you do your research—scour the Internet, go to stores, see what the point of difference is. Find out if you have an original idea or something that fits into the market. At Skip Hop we look at the market and look for the "holes"—how existing products can be improved. For example, there are lots of foam tiles out there, but they weren't safe for children ages three and under. They had choking-hazard pieces and they were ugly. So we thought, "Okay, we need to make one that is beautiful and safe." And that's how Play Spot came about.

You should also conduct focus groups and ask for advice from as many friends as you can. Take them to coffee, have them over for dessert, or just make calls. But try to get a varied group representing the range of your target consumers. We chose friends who were particular and very organized. I have this one friend, Caroline, who—to this day—brags that she bought the first Duo. She is the most organized person. So we decided Caroline is going to be the perfect tester. And then we tested it with a dad who is really nonchalant and doesn't want to be bothered with details. We wanted to make sure that people like him would like the bag, too.

There are so many organized moms' groups that you can actually meet with and give product away to or use them for focus groups. If you're willing to spare some product for testing, they're willing to help. This is a great way to avoid using expensive research firms.

Tell us about safety regulations. Is it hard to jump through the hoops?

Standards and regulations are probably keeping a lot of people from starting businesses in the baby space. There are so many regulations now with safety, content, and plastics being phthalate- and BPA [Bisphenol A] free. You have to do testing, especially if you're selling to large retailers. You have to show certificates—even to small retailers. Some of the most stringent categories are anything that has to do with feeding. Diaper bags are for parents, so the regulations are different than for products used by babies. Tabletop items and toys are strict: Items have to be a certain size so they're not choking hazards; fabric has to be tested. If you are designing a product you have to look into the cost of safety testing because it can be expensive. Every batch of products needs to be tested because these are babies we're talking about. Things have to be 100 percent safe. Products also have to go through very strict agency testing. The CPSC [Consumer Product Safety Commission] has standards. We're also members of the JPMA [Juvenile Products Manufacturers Association], which basically helps the manufacturers review those standards if they have issues with them. New companies should definitely take advantage of joining JPMA because it's a huge resource for manufacturers.

 How did you find your support networks?

We started the business at the same time as companies like Bugaboo and Oeuf. We would actually see them and other new brands at trade shows and share information. We weren't really competitors so it was complementary. We would discuss retailers or shipping methods. Most people in this business are pretty open to discussing ideas and issues—we even had a Yahoo! Group that was called "Training Wheels." We set up a message board between a few manufacturers talking about our issues with our businesses.

 How do you balance your day as a mom?

In the beginning, it was really hard. I had a babysitter help me during the day but I did a lot of stuff at night or around naps and play groups. I still wanted to experience that crazy toddler stage with my son. If you really want to do both—it means when your child is sleeping at night, the laptop goes open and you're continuing your day. I still do it. There were things I would make sure not to miss out on, like taking my son to play dates or going to classes with him. Luckily when he was young, the business wasn't the size it is now—we're thirty people; I travel a lot and have to go overseas. The stages of my son's life and the stages of my business were really terrific because they just allowed me to spend that time with him. When he was four, he even came to a trade show with us. At the end of the day I am thankful to be able to have my own business, especially with a child. You work really hard but you have the flexibility and know that you're in charge of your own schedule with no one else to answer to but yourself.

SOURCING

Whether or not you're making an edible item, it helps to think of the process of making each product like a recipe. For example, your greeting card may need one 8 ½-by-11-inch sheet of 80-pound cardstock, 12 inches of red-and-white baker's twine, and one A-7 kraft envelope. You need to gather all of the "recipes" for your products and determine what amount of each you want to create for the initial run or collection (usually just a small batch starting out). Next, make a list of all the materials along with the quantities for each. It's helpful to see if there are any materials common to your products that fall into categories, like ribbon or paper goods; that way, when you place an order for them, you can source an entire category from one vendor.

You'll benefit by sourcing your most abundant material needs from companies that offer them at wholesale cost. However, you should see what minimums (in quantity and total purchase cost) wholesalers may require. You'll have to weigh the appeal of wholesale prices against the reality of your production rate and your storage capacity. Does it make sense to get one thousand octagonal tins wholesale if you estimate selling only two hundred keepsake boxes in the next year? Remember that when you are looking at costs, the difference in quantity brackets might only be ten cents per unit; this will significantly increase your profits only if you are selling a higher volume. Sourcing always requires a bit of number crunching, so be ready to whip out the calculator to pore over every last detail.

PRODUCTION

Welcome to the world of manufacturing. Pull out your measuring stick and stopwatch because at this level it's all about precision and efficiency. Changing a little detail, like wrapping one less ribbon around a candle or using sticker labels versus tied label cards, can shave hours off your production time when you are creating products in bulk.

When you are testing out production methods, time yourself to see how long it takes to create a batch of your fabric flowers or other products you're making. Group your tasks and arrange them, assembly–line style—put together several pieces of fabric at a time and tie them in sections, for example. You may find that you can make fifty in an hour this way. You should also time someone else, since that person will most likely be less adept than you at putting together your product; having this information will help when figuring out how to pay someone should you decide to hire help in the future. But it isn't all about speed when making a product—quality counts for so much. So check the flowers to make sure they are similar in shape, size, and look; you might find that only forty-six of the fifty are perfect. You'll have to take that into consideration when you are pricing your goods (see Pricing, page 97).

EDIBLE GOODS

If your party guests are constantly impressed with your dark chocolate raspberry truffle cookies, you've probably considered the possibility of selling them. The good thing is that no customer will ever ask for a culinary school diploma before buying your cupcakes or baby food—all that matters is taste and quality. Although the food business is a place where homegrown talent can thrive, you do need a lot of practice before you begin. On top of crafting tasty recipes, you also need to know how to fix problems when they occur—like if your dough fails to rise.

Before you start, check your state's regulations and licensing requirements concerning starting a food business from your home. Some states may require you to have a commercial kitchen outside of your home (you can often rent space in a licensed kitchen at caterers' facilities, churches, or community centers), while others may allow it only if you transform your home kitchen into a commercial kitchen.

You will also need to check with your city's chamber of commerce to see if it has any special license requirements, such as a food vendor or food preparation license. The state health department may have rules governing the homemade food industry, while your local health board may need to inspect your home prior to your launch. Also, review the U.S. Food and Drug Administration's guidelines (www.fda.gov) for labeling or nutrition requirements, especially on items like baby food.

In the early days of your business, you should spend your time tweaking and perfecting recipes and getting feedback from friends and family. Indeed, taste testers should not be hard to find. You'll need to create a menu of your offerings and determine how people will get their treats from you—can they order online or just by phone? Will you ship it, hand deliver it, or make it available for customers to pick up from you? Another important consideration is packaging for your food items. You need to make sure you use packaging that helps keep it fresh and meets your state health department's criteria. If your product is organic or uses special ingredients, make sure it is labeled as such. Remember as well that your finished food product needs to be attractive, not just tasty. So your organic, homemade baby food needs to be naturally vibrant in color to reflect its freshness.

While it may be easy just to run to the nearest grocery store for supplies and ingredients to make your whoopie pies, if you'll be taking a large amount of orders you should look into commercial food suppliers. They'll provide the best prices, not to mention larger sizes, such as a 20-pound bag of flour and a 5-pound tub of butter. They may also have packaging materials (bags, bakery boxes, and plastic wrap) in bulk as well as larger commercial equipment, like mixers and trays that will allow you to make big batches. If you plan to use organic or locally grown produce in your food, consider contacting local farmers—they may be willing to support you by extending lower prices to you, especially if you'll be listing the name of their farm on your packaging or Web site.

PACKAGING

It's important that every detail of your packaging expresses the message you want to put out about your product and brand. Pairing a slick, glossy box with natural, hand-dyed coasters sends mixed messages, in essence neutralizing the branding of your product. Whether you choose a simple cellophane bag or an elaborate, hinged cardboard box, the packaging will be where customers absorb information about the product that will help to seal the deal. When creating your products' packaging, think about these considerations:

→ While your packaging should enhance your product, it shouldn't cost more or be more complicated than what it houses.

→ Make sure the label gives clear, succinct descriptions about the product and how to use it, if the product's use is not immediately discernable. Include the ingredients or materials used, because people may have allergies to things like nuts or wool. The labels should also be printed with eye-catching graphics and legible type.

→ Create packaging that makes it easy for your retailer to display the product. For example, in our experience with stationery, retailers generally liked boxed note cards because they can stand on their own. Making an item as store friendly as possible is key.

→ Packaging can also be a means to protect your product and ensure it gets to the end user in perfect condition. For example, if your ceramic diffuser can topple over with sticks inside, it should probably be housed in a container that keeps it upright and protects it from being damaged.

→ Keep your packaging as light as possible. If you're packaging your jewelry in heavy glass jars, shipping will cost more. Passing those shipping costs to your retailers might result in a cancellation or a request to get rid of the jars.

For a one-mom business, you might come to find outsourcing to be your most efficient and economical option. As strong as the urge might be, dyeing fibers by hand might not be as profitable as having someone else do that for you. Many designers choose local sewing businesses or manufacturers because of the convenience of being able to check in on the production process as well as the ability to retrieve the products as soon as they're ready. You can outsource part of your product-making process, such as hiring a printing press to cut and score your greeting cards, or outsource the whole thing, such as hiring an overseas factory to make the entire product from start to finish along with packaging. To find vendors, both locally and internationally based, we recommend attending trade shows—you'll get to talk to representatives in person, plus you'll get to see samples of their work.

PRICING

It doesn't matter how delectable your lemon cheesecake bars are; it doesn't matter that you sell out your entire stash of bars every week at the farmers' market; if you don't set a price for them that covers your costs and earns you a proper profit, your business will eventually fail. Pricing is paramount. When thinking about your pricing, you'll have to consider these key factors:

》→ How much does it cost you to make and package your product (the break-even point)?

》→ How much profit do you want to make?

》→ Do you want to sell at both the wholesale and retail levels?

》→ What does your competition charge?

》→ What are customers willing to pay?

Because every business is different, no single pricing formula will fit all needs. Your formula can take into account product costs like materials and labor, promotional costs like advertising, and fixed costs like equipment and utilities. When you create a formula, consider your production method as well—do you make the products in a batch or individually? How much of a wage do you want to make for the time it takes you to make your product (including any delivery time, if necessary)? The following is a basic pricing formula; use it as a basis to develop your own:

Sample Pricing Formula for a Cupcake

Let's say the cost of materials (flour, butter, sugar, chocolate, liners, and so on) for a batch of 24 cupcakes is $1.50. Overhead costs are estimated at $0.25. It takes 1 hour of labor to make and package the 24 cupcakes and your labor cost is $20 an hour. (Note: The standard markup for your wholesale price is 100 percent, or multiplying by 2, over cost. The same markup applies to establishing retail prices as well.)

Product cost (break-even)

Materials + Labor + Overhead ÷ Number of Units = Price

($1.50 + $0.25 + $20.00) ÷ 24 = $0.90 per cupcake

Wholesale price (if sold to restaurants or retailers)

Cost per item x 2: $0.90 x 2 = $1.80 per cupcake

Your profit margin at the wholesale rate is $0.90 per cupcake.

Retail price (if sold directly to the consumer)

Wholesale price x 2: $1.80 x 2 = $3.60 per cupcake

Your profit margin at the retail rate is $2.70 per cupcake.

If you plug away at your formula and find that your price is lower than your competitors' prices, you may consider bringing yours up to increase your profit margin, or keeping it low to remain competitive. If your price is coming out much higher than your competitors', see if there's anything special about your product that warrants its price tag, or find a way to increase your efficiency (reducing labor costs) without compromising quality so you can bring down the price.

WHOLESALE BASICS

If you can build wholesale into your product's pricing structure, it means you can sell to shops and restaurants—opening up another market for your product. Wholesale is the process of selling your products at a lower cost, in bulk, and without sales tax to retailers. The definition of bulk is up to you—it can mean three pillows or a thousand pillows. Below are some of the elements you'll need in order to communicate with the wholesale market.

Terms. When retailers want to buy your products, they'll want to know your terms—what types of payment you will accept from them. Generally, companies accept credit cards (see Merchant Account, page 125), business checks, PayPal, collect on delivery (COD), or a delayed payment, typically within thirty days (called "Net 30"). Typically, you should extend Net 30 terms to your customers only after they've placed (and paid for) at least two orders. Although extending credit may help you build a relationship with your retailers, it's inherently risky and will require you to chase payment, on unpaid invoices. However, if a larger retail store like Anthropologie places an order requesting Net 30 right off the bat, then it would obviously be to your benefit to extend credit to them.

Resale tax form. When you offer wholesale cost to a company, you need to be sure that it is a valid retailer. To verify that it is exempt from paying you sales tax, you will need to create a simple form that collects its resale information, including legal name (as opposed to the "doing business as" [DBA] name), address of record, and reseller license number.

Minimums. To establish a floor for purchases and to prevent retailers from making personal purchases, you should set minimums for a buyer's initial and subsequent orders. Your opening order minimum may be $150, while your reorder minimum may be $100 (ongoing orders are usually lower). You can also set a minimum per product style. Requiring a minimum order of four of your block-printed tote bags might help to give your products a greater presence and selection in the shops.

Lead time. We always notify retailers of lead times to fulfill orders, especially for custom orders. Create a buffer for your lead time, especially during seasons when you would expect multiple orders, such as at a trade show or around the holidays. Regardless of whether your product is ready to ship right away, always ask retailers when they'd like to receive the shipment. They might be limited in their storage capacity or may be buying product to sell during a certain season.

Catalog. It's likely that the word *catalog* evokes an image of the J.Crew glossy you get in the mail. But when you're starting out, you don't need anything that complicated to intrigue your buyers. It can be as simple as a large postcard with images of your product, a printed twelve-page booklet, or even a simple PDF version of the latter. Unlike a J.Crew catalog, wholesale catalogs show only the merchandise. Save pricing, minimums, and net terms for your line sheet.

Line sheets. Line sheets spell out the ordering details of the products found in your catalog, including product names, item numbers, and price. They also need to inform retailers of the minimum order requirements, terms, lead times, and shipping and return policies (See Shipping and Fulfillment, page 132). They can often be created to double as order forms.

APPROACHING RETAILERS

Shop owners genuinely love checking out new products and supporting new talent—it's vital for their business. But barging into a shop and demanding to show three cases of feather earrings is not the way to a shopkeeper's heart. Always call or e-mail ahead of time and politely ask for an appointment. If they don't have time, ask if you could send a catalog, line sheet, business card, and even a sample or two for their consideration. Follow up in a week with a short but sweet note. It's also important to keep in mind that buyers may have retail buying cycles—often related to trade show schedules and shopping seasons. So even if your woolen llama made the owner shriek with joy, she might not place an order right away, if it's not the right time in her buying schedule. You may want to check back later or ask if she'd like to place an order for a later delivery, like before the holiday season.

ECO-FRIENDLY PRODUCTS

Healthy living and reducing our carbon footprint has become a focus of our society in the past few years, and products made with materials or processes that are conscious of the environment are now the new norm. Products claiming to be eco-friendly cover a broad spectrum—from some that simply have one "green" component to others that go the distance and are made entirely with materials from eco-certified vendors. You'll need to be specific about how your product is green: Is the paper you're using made of 30 percent postconsumer waste (PCW) or 100 percent PCW? Make this clear in your product description instead of merely saying "recycled paper." And make sure you're not sending mixed messages either, like packaging your bamboo utensil set in a plastic container.

The easiest way to show that your product is legitimately eco-friendly is to get it certified through third-party companies like EcoLogo or Green Seal. If your product passes such a company's certification process (fees apply), you'll get an insignia to put on both your site and your product. These details will boost the authenticity of your brand and legitimize your company philosophy.

RETAIL SALES

Nowadays, a designer who roots her business in wholesale can also concurrently have a Web site that offers her products for direct sale and even participate in retail shows that sell directly to the public. If you choose to offer your products directly to consumers, remember to charge prices that are comparable to what your stores are charging for the same products. Do not undercut your retailers by offering your custom melamine plates at the wholesale price to the general public—this will undermine and possibly end your relationship with your retailers. For more information on setting up an online shop, go to chapter 5, page 110, and for information on selling at a retail show, see page 103.

TRADE SHOWS

A trade show is like the big time for any product designer, a veritable *Star Trek* convention of sorts, and there are trade shows for almost every interest imaginable—from toys and stationery to soap and jewelry. It's where many companies go to launch their product or brands, and it's only open to the trade (vendors or store owners) and press. Trade shows are held in metropolitan cities worldwide—New York and Las Vegas are home to some notable ones like the New York International Gift Show and the fashion trade show Magic in Las Vegas. You'll have to decide which shows are best for capturing your market. Talk to other business owners or check online forums for feedback to see which shows appear to be the most lucrative. Note also that participating in trade shows can mean that you're on the road for several days or even a week, so you'll also want to consider your family's needs and schedules—paying special attention to determining who will care for your child while you are away.

Before you apply for a show, you should figure out whether your budget will allow it, as the cost of the booth, displays, samples, marketing, and travel can run well into the thousands. Also, do you have enough of a collection to fill up an 8-by-10-foot booth? If not, you should ask the show management if they are open to exhibitors sharing a booth. You'll have to find a company to partner with, but this is a good solution for companies with smaller collections—not to mention the fact that it reduces the booth fee expenses. If you are accepted into a show, check out where your booth is located and who your booth neighbors will be as early as possible. If it seems far from the main traffic or you're positioned next to a questionable company, ask the show managers to move your booth.

Trade shows take a lot of planning. For one, you need to design a booth that will draw in buyers and press. You also need to have a pre-show marketing plan to make your booth a buyers' destination. First, you'll need to create a list of buyers—you may be able to acquire or buy this from show management. Otherwise, if you visit previous exhibitors' Web sites (find companies similar to yours), you can find this information on their list of retailers. You can also make a list of newspaper and magazine editors; pick up copies of the publications and collect the editors' names and addresses from the mastheads. When you've compiled your list, send them a postcard or mailing that includes basic information about your business, your contact info, and, most important, your booth location. Consider including an incentive to order during the show, like 20 percent off their order or free shipping for orders over $200. Many buyers walk the entire show floor first—taking note of which booths they're interested in—and then return later to closely inspect booths and make their purchases. Offering fun little things such as food, candy, or a small giveaway (like a tote bag) helps buyers remember you as they make their list of booths to revisit.

RETAIL SHOWS

Retail shows, such as craft fairs and farmers' markets, often have a more intimate feel than trade shows do. Instead of standing on cold concrete floors, you might be setting up over dirt or grass. Frequency and timing vary: farmers' markets may happen every Saturday, fairs like the Renegade Craft Fair take place during a weekend once or twice a year in a city, and retail shows like the Holiday Shops at Bryant Park in New York City last six weeks or more. Unlike at trade shows, you'll sell directly to the customer, so prepare for cash-and-carry and even set yourself up to take credit cards. The best part of participating in a retail show is that it allows you to interact with your customer. You'll get instant feedback and validation, in the form of compliments and sales.

You'll need to amass enough inventory to last the entire show. If it's your first show, it may be hard to determine what this magic amount should be. A good rule of thumb is to bring more than you think you need—products are easier to sell when tables look full. An empty booth looks like it's been picked over and discourages buyers from coming in to explore. When displaying, keep it simple and remember to always highlight your merchandise. Don't display your wool throws in an elaborate armoire if you think the armoire might steal the spotlight from the product you're selling.

TRADE AND RETAIL SHOW CHECKLIST

- **Products.** Of course, you'll need your products to sell or to put on display. It's also helpful to bring backup products. For example, Cat brings an extra set of her most important products in her carry-on just in case freight is delayed.

- **Marketing materials.** Arm yourself with marketing handouts like business cards, postcards, and press kits as well as promotional displays like a magazine article featuring your product.

- **Technicals.** Do you need to sign up and pay for electrical or installation of walls, lights, or flooring? If you plan on using your laptop, check for Internet access and available electrical outlets.

- **Freight and transportation.** Will you be using UPS, a freight company, or hauling it in your hatchback? Note that shows often have separate deadlines for shipping items in advance.

- **Signage.** Too often, the tell-tale sign of a newbie exhibitor is the lack of a prominent signage. Make sure the name of your company and booth number is displayed in several locations including the back and sidewalls as well as on any tables.

- **Payment or order collection.** For retail shows, are you set up to take credit cards or do you have a cash box stocked with bills and coins? Bring a calculator as well as receipt books for easy transactions. For trade shows, carbon copy invoices with company information, clipboards, staplers, and pens are helpful.

- **Rescue and respite items.** You will be on your feet, standing on concrete or dirt and beneath hot lights or exposed to outdoor elements. Be sure to wear comfortable shoes, layered clothing, and have snacks, mints, and drinks stashed beneath your table.

- **Booth rescue items.** Bring a small box filled with double-sided tape, duct tape, scissors, a needle and thread, Velcro, a screwdriver, the tools of your craft, and other "repair" items.

- **Clever storage.** Many exhibitors plan meticulously for the breakdown of their booth so they can make a swift exit to escape the swell of herds. Think about using your rollaway luggage, paper bags, or canvas bins that can collapse and pop up with ease.

- **Travel and accommodations.** Book your plane tickets or reserve your truck rental well in advance of a show. For trade shows, check first with the travel agencies affiliated with the show, as they will likely have the best rates for rooms during that time.

- **Child care.** Have you made arrangements with your spouse or for a sitter while you're away? If you plan to bring your child with you to the show, check first with show management to see if children are allowed on the floor. If so, be prepared to bring a table as well as a barrage of activities to keep them busy.

To a busy mom lassoed to schedules, the idea of a sales representative who will pound the pavement for you may sound like a dream. Sales reps cover various territories, such as all of southeast Michigan, or a specific urban center like New York City, so they know the retailers in their area and have nurtured relationships with them over the years. In return for representation, you are expected to pay a commission, typically 15 percent, for any sale that occurs in their territory. That means that if you get an order via e-mail from a store in your rep's territory, you will owe your rep a commission, whether or not she was responsible for making the sale.

 To a busy mom lassoed to schedules, the idea of a sales representative who will pound the pavement for you may sound like a dream.

A *showroom rep* is part of a larger company that has a main showroom where they display products and invite retailers to visit. They also participate in trade shows. Many will require a fee to display your goods in their showroom as well as a fee to cover marketing and participation in trade shows. An *independent rep* usually carries smaller product lines and relies heavily on going door-to-door to shops in their territory. Before you try to find a rep, it's important to note that they are very selective. They usually favor lines with varied or multiple offerings, as well as companies who have proven sales records and interest from retailers.

DWELLSTUDIO
Modern Home Accessories
New York, New York

According to Christiane Lemieux, the tools you need to start your business could already be inside you—that is, if you choose a business that capitalizes on the skills, experience, and contacts you've made along the way. With a go-with-what-you've-got mentality, Christiane started Dwell-Studio—and what she had were surface design skills, experience in home accessories, and contacts with factories to fulfill her ideas. All those elements proved to be a recipe for success in carrying out her plan to fill a void in the home accessories market in 1999—a niche in modern textiles. Twelve years later, Christiane stands at the helm of a burgeoning home-furnishings empire—including licensing deals with Target, Tiny Prints, Robert Allen, and Precedent Furniture, among others—which will now encompass a full lifestyle experience by expanding into furniture.

Q *What led you to start DwellStudio?*

I graduated from Parsons The New School for Design in 1997 with a degree in fashion design. My first job was as a textile designer for Isaac Mizrahi and later an assistant fashion designer for The Gap. But surface design remained my interest. I had the excellent opportunity to work for an amazing home furnishings company called Portico. That job threw me into the home furnishings and accessories world. At Portico, I was able to try my hand at everything from furniture design to fragrance formulation. It was the perfect learning environment for me. It also helped me hone my style and find my place in the market. So just as a fashion designer's assistant leaves with all the tools to start her own line, I left with direct experience in the home accessories industry along with some contacts, including overseas factories. Since they knew me, they even offered my company Net 30 terms [thirty-day delayed payment on invoices] right off the bat. I took all the knowledge I had accumulated and used that to start my company. I saw an opportunity in the marketplace—and luckily I also had the skill set and the contacts to carry out that opportunity. It's always good to start a business in the industry where your skill set and knowledge lie—then there won't be much of a learning curve.

 Describe the early days launching DwellStudio. What was it like? When did you hire your first employee?

For six months I operated out of my living room. But I had to get an office; if you're going to meet with people in the industry, press, or retailers, you need an office for legitimacy. When I moved to the new office, Jennifer Chused came on board. The place did not have any heat and doubled as our showroom. So during the winter months we couldn't even stay there long! There were four of us originally: me, Jennifer, a salesperson, and a part-time bookkeeper. Back then I did everything—changed the lightbulbs, took out the garbage, bookkeeping, human resources, sales, design . . . I was a one-woman team.

The good thing is the larger we got, the more focused everyone's work became. The multitaskers are freed up to do what they're best at. A company of specialists is always going to be better than a company of generalists. If people are focused on what they are good at, the better the company will be at executing their goals—and it translates into the product. In the beginning, you can't afford top-level people, but you can hire people who are excited and willing to try anything—and over time you'll find out what they're good at.

 What are your responsibilities now?

My main responsibilities are design and marketing. People always wonder if I'm really blogging and tweeting—and it really is me! It is authentic and it's helped give the company a personality.

Q *Did being a mother inspire any new products or styles at DwellStudio?*

We were already doing a children's product line before I had children. We had a niche in the home market and extended that modern look to baby. But now we can use our own experiences as parents to inspire products. If it's something we could really use, we think, "Why don't we just design it?" For example, when we'd take our kids to a restaurant, we were always lugging a giant backpack full of stuff. So we came up with the Scribble Kit that included a scribble pad and crayons—and it's been a great product. So having a kid has helped us figure out what's necessary because there's so much unnecessary stuff out there right now for kids. At the end of the day, you don't need a lot. You just need the fundamentals.

Q *How did having your children, Isabelle and William, affect how you worked?*

I didn't get a three-month maternity leave. I literally took four days off. Juggling—well, you just do what you have to do. I don't get to the office at 9:00 A.M. like I used to; it's more like 10:00 A.M. now. And I work till 5:00 P.M. so I'm home in time to give my children a bath and dinner. I start work again at 8:30 P.M. and do as much as I can before I fall asleep. I don't get as many uninterrupted hours to work—and your day is more fragmented.

Q *How has having your own business enriched your family life?*

It's been tremendous. We have so much flexibility. We can go on vacation together without having to clear it by anyone. If I need to volunteer and read a book to Isabelle's class, I can. When my son, William, was an infant, he had colic—and the doctor recommended that he be asleep by 5:00 P.M. to cure it. So for a month, I would leave the office by 4:30 P.M. to get him to bed by 5:00 P.M. Now, if I had a banking or legal job in New York, I doubt I could do that! As an employer, I extend this flexibility to everyone, especially parents, who work here. I am completely supportive of them leaving by 5:00 P.M. I understand the juggle, so I have a tremendous amount of empathy for the parents who work here.

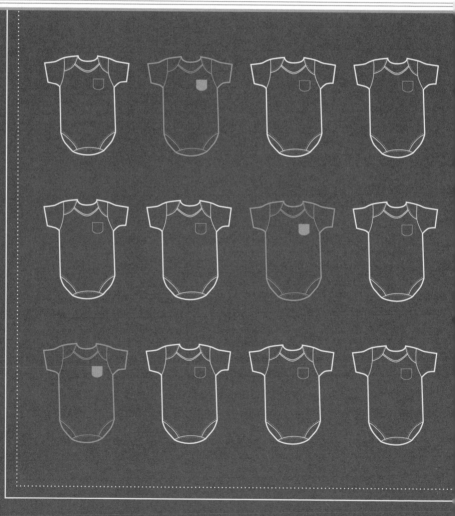

opening
AN ONLINE RETAIL SHOP

chapter

05

Our RETAIL REVERIE goes back to our days as children—when we would gather up our playthings and arrange them among tables and shelves so our customers (a.k.a. siblings) could peruse the selection in our "toy store." Having a store no longer has to be make-believe; these days, you can start and manage an ONLINE SHOP FROM YOUR HOME. You get to flex your creative muscle crafting the type of store you want, selecting the products you will offer, and designing your site—all processes we'll cover in this chapter. If you're looking to COMBINE YOUR PASSION WITH A BUSINESS and love interacting with customers every day, then BEING A SHOPKEEPER may have been your life's calling all along.

LIFE AS AN ONLINE SHOP OWNER

Compared to a brick-and-mortar shopkeeper, you'll have it easy. You won't have to worry about manning it, as your shop will be open around the clock, taking in orders from around the country (or the world) even while you sleep. There will be no risk of theft, and you won't have to mull over your store window display. You'll have a greater profit margin because of less overhead (no lease or utilities) and operational costs (no liability insurance or employee wages). And you can market your products

 You'll have a greater profit margin because of less overhead (no lease or utilities) and operational costs (no liability insurance or employee wages).

by showing customers recent press coverage, as well as describing your products in greater depth. But it won't all be like living on Easy Street. Unlike a traditional storefront, competition will be fierce, not to mention global. You do need to figure out the technical details of running the site professionally and offering a secure shopping experience. You will have to design the look of the shop and offer photographs and written descriptions of your merchandise. You won't be able to simply hang an "open" sign and just expect people to come through your "doors"—you'll have to litter the Internet with links to your site so that customers can find you.

YOUR IDEAL SHOP

You never forget your first business. For Meg, her foray into entrepreneurship kicked off with a bustling online shop selling wedding invitations and accessories. For you, it could be a children's clothing shop that sells only pajamas, an Etsy shop that offers vintage scarves and brooches, or a home accessories shop that sells Swedish product lines. The number and variety of niche shops you can devise are endless. When you begin to brainstorm, a good place to start is with a field you love, since you will spend plenty of hours in this environment. Consider pragmatic issues as well: If you call a one-bedroom apartment home, selling vintage jewelry will make more sense than offering bulky home accessories. And can your vendor in Sweden restock your cuckoo clocks in time before you sell out? If your shop relies on nontraditional, distant, or hard-to-get items, you'll have to be extra diligent about ordering early or making regular trips to sources.

FINDING AND BUYING PRODUCTS

You may have noticed that being a mom has made you somewhat of an expert shopper. As moms, we are avid comparison shoppers (reading reviews of strollers and playpens) and are more conscious of the products

 Think of this job as equal parts shopper, curator, forecaster, and scavenger.

we give to our children than we ever were with ourselves! This discriminating eye will help you be a savvy buyer for your shop. Think of this job as equal parts shopper, curator, forecaster, and scavenger. As a buyer, you'll have to consider price points, minimum quantities, terms, and delivery dates. In your curatorial role, you'll be picking items that create a specific thumbprint for your shop. Forecasting means factoring in the seasons when certain products would sell best. And as a scavenger, you'll have to keep your eyes open at all times—searching high and low for the right products or, better yet, discovering something that no other shop carries. Where should you begin your search for items to sell? Start here:

No. 1 BLOGS

Dig through blogs and chase links to artists or designers who may interest you. Contact them to request a catalog, wholesale order form, and line sheet. If the artist doesn't have any of these items, be creative and strike a deal with him—maybe he'll be interested in creating his porcelain bear figurines exclusively for your shop.

No. 2 LOCAL BOUTIQUES

Local shops may carry products made by local artists that aren't sold elsewhere. Have a notepad handy so you can write down any pertinent information to help you contact the maker. It's important to be discreet when you do this, especially if you're trying to capture a photo of the object with your phone.

No. 3 TRADE SHOWS

Want to be dizzy with options? Products abound at trade shows, which take place in major market areas like New York, Chicago, San Francisco, or Las Vegas (see Resources, page 202). It's like getting a backstage pass to view and touch new products before they hit store shelves, not to mention the fact that you'll also get to meet the people behind some companies. You'll want to scour every inch of a trade show, so bring comfy shoes and a tote bag for catalogs. If you want to take photographs of products, be sure to get the company's permission first. Have business cards ready since you'll have to exchange yours for any catalogs and line sheets.

When you're ready to place an order with a company, it's important to know that it's possible to negotiate the terms of your order. If you're unsure if a product is a good fit for you, ask if they'd be willing to reduce their minimum and sell you a smaller amount. This will allow you to test a product without building up too much inventory. You can also indicate when you want your order to be shipped. If it's May, but you don't need the order until the holiday season, instruct them to ship it in November. When possible, request that companies extend credit to you by offering terms (delaying payment from fifteen to ninety days).

INVENTORY PLANNING

As the adage goes, "you can't sell from an empty cart." It's true; stores are often more appealing when they're stocked with a variety of products. This is where the fun begins: making a list of the products that will line your store's "shelves" and then organizing them into categories. Your eco-friendly gift shop could be divided into sections like books, art, stationery, children's, bath and body, clothing, and jewelry. Jot down each product's prices as well to ensure you have a good range of price points to offer. After figuring out the range of your products, you need to estimate how many of each you need to order. This combination will help you determine your ideal opening inventory. A shopkeeper's primary goal and challenge is to maintain just enough merchandise and turn it over as quickly as possible to recover the tied-up capital. Getting to know the buying habits of her regular customers has helped Cat determine how much inventory to keep in stock for her boutique. Over time you will learn to make adjustments to your buying schedule to keep the right amount of inventory.

PRICING

Without a doubt, no other business model is more familiar than retail. The concept is quite simple: *If you buy an item for $5, sell it for $10.* The standard retail practice is a 100 percent markup over the wholesale

Price also makes a statement about the quality of the product.

price. If you think that reducing the markup (buying an item for $5 and selling for $7) will make it more enticing to customers, you're assuming that customers buy on price alone—a false notion that many businesses believe and act on. While no one can resist a good deal, chances are that your friends aren't wearing the cheapest shirts they could find. Although price was something they considered when purchasing that shirt, it was not the ultimate deciding factor.

Price your products appropriately with an ample markup—match the manufacturer's suggested retail (often double the wholesale cost) or even add a little more to help offset credit card fees and packaging and shipping costs, and to buffer for a markdown. Oftentimes, manufacturers may not allow or will look unfavorably upon shops that apply discounts to their suggested retail. Price also makes a statement about the quality of the product. If you price a product too low, people may wonder, "What's wrong with it?" Overprice it and you may find yourself having a hard time explaining the price or fielding too many complaints from customers.

THREE POTATO FOUR

Online Shop, Vintage Housewares
Philadelphia, Pennsylvania

Nestled among buildings in an old wool mill in the Northern Manayunk area of Philadelphia sits Janet Morales at her dream job: co-owner of Three Potato Four, a vintage retail shop she shares with her husband, Stu Eli. It's a far cry from their life six years prior, a busy, work-consumed existence in the graphic design industry in New York. The catalyst for this change? The birth of their daughter, Holly, in 2005. With her arrival, neither of them could see the point of working hard only to arrive home and watch her go to sleep. Janet remarks, "We had a beautiful baby, but no time for her. We were missing out on her babyhood." When Holly was eight months old, Janet was laid off—and it was just what she needed. Stu was also feeling the pull to be at home, and they both started thinking of having their own business. Janet's story shows how having children can cause you to reprioritize your life and focus on what matters most. With that focus, they've been able to pull in sales from around the world and receive constant editorial coverage from esteemed publications such as *Dwell*, *ReadyMade*, and *Martha Stewart Living*.

 When you knew that you wanted to start a business, what were the first steps you took?

My parents wanted us to move near them in northern Virginia, so they could help us out more with Holly. We thought it was a good idea considering we wanted to start a business, so we moved there. While we were still trying to figure out what business we'd do, Stu took a job at a design firm for six months until he quit to launch the business. We were scared, but we figured it was the best time considering we had the help from my parents.

What led you to choose opening an online vintage shop?

In the beginning, our thought was to start a brick-and-mortar shop. We considered a stationery shop and even a burger shop! But then we thought about what we loved most—and Stu and I love collecting things. Both of our families are big into collecting antiques. You can almost say it's in our blood. My mom is a collector of Victorian flowery stuff. I actually didn't appreciate it growing up when she'd take me on Virginia back roads to go antiquing. Stu's dad is a big coin collector—he'd take Stu to flea markets and coin swaps. Those experiences have actually helped us in forming our interests and even how we pick objects for the shop.

 How did you come up with the name Three Potato Four?

When Holly was two, we were trying to teach her to sleep in her own bed. We were saying the "One potato, two potato" rhyme to her every night. This was around the same time we were thinking of a name for our business, too. It occurred to us that it was kind of catchy. So we went online to see if the domain name was taken—and "One Potato Two Potato" was, but "Three Potato Four" was not. We love the name—it's playful and easy to remember. It also sends a message that we don't take ourselves too seriously. And it's also one of those names that makes you smile because there's a childhood memory attached to it. In that sense, it works as a name for a vintage shop.

 How do you find the objects you sell in your shop?

We go to a lot of auctions, antique markets, antique shops, and flea markets, and occasionally Stu goes on "picking trips"—which sometimes includes trips to abandoned schools or barns on the East Coast. We've also made a lot of contacts with antique dealers; sometimes they call us to tell us about a factory or a barn that we can pick through.

Since we both come from a graphic design background, we're attracted to things with type and great color—so we find ourselves picking up old signage pieces quite frequently. In addition, we're often drawn to everyday utilitarian items from schools, libraries, science labs, and public works. We also have a strong affinity for items from old general stores, bakeries, and candy shops. Above all else, we try to look for unique pieces that you wouldn't necessarily find at any regular antique shop. We also look for things that have a bit of humor or things that can be repurposed—like conveyer belt trays or wooden boxes from an old shoe factory.

What makes your online shop different from others that sell vintage wares?

We're a mom-and-pop shop, so we try to emphasize and build our brand on that. It's a small family business and we want the customer to know that there are actual people behind it. This permeates everything, from the photography to customer service to the daily entries of our personal life via all of our social media outlets (like Facebook, Twitter, and our blog). We also strive to get across to the consumer that these are hand-picked items that we've scoured the country for—that the items each have a story behind them, making them unique. We also drive the site with our photography; we spend a lot of time styling the products for the shots. We really want people to get the sense of what the object would look like in their house.

How has your shop changed during the past three years? What do you see in the years to come?

We recently moved to Philadelphia. We wanted to open a brick-and-mortar store and Pennsylvania is really good for antiques. It's been interesting having a physical shop and balancing it with the online one. We started out with regular hours, but we've changed that. It was getting hard to keep hours and to maintain the site. If we sold something in the shop, we'd have to remember to take it off the site. We were struggling to keep it updated and to keep both stocked. So we decided to have "barn sales," or monthly sales, instead of keeping the shop open all the time. Opening the store is more of an event now. It allows us to have more time to go to the market or on picking trips. Going forward, we also want to come out with our own products that are vintage inspired. We always sell so many great one-off things that it would be great to have more of them and give them a modern spin.

Your online shop inches toward reality once you secure a domain name. As it relies solely on Web traffic, your outpost on the Internet needs a domain that is memorable, not too cumbersome, and easy to type. To that end, avoid having one with too many dashes, and try your best to get one that ends in ".com," since that is most people's expectation.

Next, think about the overall look and design of your shop, as this is essential for your branding (see Establishing an Original Brand, page 136). Meander through online shops you enjoy and take note of elements you

As it relies solely on Web traffic, your outpost on the Internet needs a domain that is memorable, not too cumbersome, and easy to type.

like. Because first impressions are everything, the first page of your site (also called the index page) must be carefully planned. It should be inviting but not overwhelming. When shoppers arrive at your site, they need a little time and space to orient themselves before they are barraged with information and choices. Customers need time to look around and get the lay of the land. Your goal should be to give customers a comfortable and enjoyable experience, because the longer a shopper remains in your store (or on your site), the more likely she is to buy. As a rule of thumb, remember that it is better to have a simple, up-to-date online shop than a complex, ambitious one that isn't maintained well.

The infrastructure of your site will influence a slew of issues, from how to accept credit cards to how you ship orders. If you have a hard time making a decision about an e-commerce platform, ask around for references. As long as you ask a shop owner who isn't in direct competition with you, you'll find that some will be forthcoming about the system they're using. When it's time to start building your site, you have several options to choose from.

Design a Web site from scratch and implement e-commerce software. A Web site with a few Paypal buttons just barely meets the criteria for an online store. Unless you're simply selling a handful of items, a site like this won't be very useful to you. A good online store should employ e-commerce software that offers an easy-to-use shopping cart and checkout system, automated e-mail to customers, and inventory management tools. Unless you are a designer with Web programming skills, it would be to your benefit to hire one—because a homemade online shop isn't as endearing as a homemade cookie. If it looks like your kid cousin hooked up your shop in his spare time, people may be reluctant to enter their credit card information. So find a designer who fits your aesthetic, but be prepared to pay for high-quality work. A basic site with eight to ten pages can cost anywhere from $1,000 to $10,000 and beyond depending on the designer and the amount of pages and functionality you want. When you sit down with a designer, check to see whether he or she works with a programmer or expects you to find one, because this will affect the overall cost. Work with your Web site programmer to determine which e-commerce system would work best.

Get everything you need in an all-in-one store solution. Many services such as Yahoo! Merchant Solutions and Big Cartel are one-stop shops for your online store, offering design templates, hosting, and a built-in e-commerce system. The definition of "all-in-one" varies among e-commerce solutions—some have more to offer with regard to merchandising (such as suggesting related products), shopping cart functions (perhaps offering a subtotal, shipping cost estimates, tax and discount calculation, and gift message option), and the number of products you can list for sale. Order management is often easier; some provide tools for tracking inventory and processing orders, returns, and exchanges. Some offer marketing measurement tools like traffic statistics; others provide an invoice database compatible with accounting programs like QuickBooks. Yahoo! Merchant Solutions and other systems also include a shipping tool that can produce a label with your customer's information. All these systems have fees commensurate with the types of perks they provide. Most offer a trial period, so take them out for a test drive and mess around with the controls and features before you commit.

Get a storefront in a marketplace. Equal parts online community and sales device, marketplaces provide sellers with a storefront and a built-in membership of buyers. Do some research before committing, because some have restrictions that might not align with your goals. At Etsy (www.etsy.com), you can sell products handmade by you, craft supplies, or vintage items that are at least twenty years old. Supermarket (SuperMarketHQ.com) is typically for artists and designers who create their own products, while Bonanza (www.bonanza.com) allows you to sell just about anything under the sun. The advantages are numerous with a marketplace: Your inventory is automatically entered into their searchable database, product pages are social-media friendly (pages can be instantly "liked" on Facebook or embedded into a tweet), and they have a streamlined shopping system so you don't have to apply for a merchant account. Despite being an easy, low-cost solution to launch a shop, it isn't for everyone. Being a part of a marketplace makes it more difficult to be an individual brand, especially since you won't have your own domain name, and matching storefront formats can make everyone seem the same. They also mix a variety of sellers (from professional businesses to hobbyists), so it's not good for someone who's gearing up her shop to be high-end.

QUALITIES OF A SUCCESSFUL ONLINE SHOP

Like a traditional storefront, your online store needs constant maintenance. In the world of online shopping, you'll quickly learn that there is no shortage of annoying glitches that can occur—and as a shopkeeper you have to stay on top of them.

Online Shop Checklist

>> A memorable, easy-to-type domain name

>> A Web site that is professional looking and attractively designed

>> Easy navigation around the site (requiring the least amount of guessing for the customer to find what she wants)

>> Products arranged by category to help customers find items more easily

>> Categories, such as "new products," created only when you have enough products to fill them and keep current

>> Good product photographs including detail shots and scale

>> Clear product descriptions written with your brand's tone

>> Product pages with an obvious buy button

>> Ample "white space" (areas without pattern or text) to make the type readable

>> Large enough type for people to read

>> Easy checkout (it's clear which fields are required and customers receive few or no error messages)

>> New products added to the site regularly to keep customers coming back (at least monthly, if not weekly)

>> Links to product alternatives provided

More than just a place to hawk your wares, Etsy is an active, world-wide community. As long as you're selling vintage goods (twenty years or older), crafting supplies, or handmade goods that you created yourself, Etsy will provide you with a storefront to list your goods. Naturally, there are fees, but they eliminate the burden of setting up an e-commerce system and getting a merchant account. With a philosophy based on empowering individuals to connect with each other, they've become a selling powerhouse, amassing, in just seven years, more than 400,00 sellers that reach a membership of five million eager buyers.

Danielle Maveal is Etsy's seller education coordinator. She manages the blog, newsletter, and live workshops geared toward providing sellers with the tools and information to be successful. Danielle suggests that sellers offer as many photos as they can for each product and that the photos should grab people's attention. While having a picture of a necklace floating in white space works for many online shops, at Etsy, shoppers prefer warm and less-edited photos. Danielle stresses that product descriptions should "tell your buyers a story." Etsy buyers are not like just any buyers—they're looking for handmade or vintage objects that speak to them and they want to buy them from a seller who they believe in and trust. Trust is solidified further when sellers are visible members of the online community. Being active in social networks like Facebook and Twitter or joining a local Etsy team will help you connect with others and build community. Etsy sellers are known for providing customer service that "blows away all other online retailers," says Danielle. They respond quickly to customer inquiries and many orders have been known to arrive looking like presents, adorned with ribbon and even a hand-written note.

MERCHANT ACCOUNT

For online store owners, money is not the paper stuff you find in your wallet, but data transfers from customer credit card transactions. How do you start accepting them? Unless you are opening a storefront in a marketplace like Bonanza or using Paypal as your checkout gateway, you'll need to set up a merchant account. Merchant accounts accept and hold money from credit card transactions, which is later deposited into your bank account. These accounts can be set up through merchant service providers like banks or independent providers (like Authorize.net or Verisign). Check with your e-commerce provider to see which merchant service providers are compatible with its payment processing system. Signing up for one usually requires a review of your credit since there is always a built-in risk associated with online shops (physical cards are not present to scan). Read the fine print in the schedule of setup fees, monthly fees, per-transaction fees, discount rates (percentage of total sales fees), and charge-back fees (when disputes are settled in favor of the credit card holder). Many of these fees can be negotiated—if you shop around, you can request that one merchant service provider match the fees of another.

SALES POLICIES

Online shopping is founded on trust: Customers make a purchase based on the belief that they're getting the product as it was described on your site. This trust can be solidified through your sales policies. The most important policies to institute are the shipping, exchange, and return policies. Post these terms prominently on your site, or, better yet, make customers acknowledge them at checkout.

Shipping. You have to be clear about where you can ship orders and how long it will take to process and deliver them. Can you ship orders to any country in the world, to a select few, or just within the United States? How long will it take you to process an order before it ships? Do you send out shipments only on Wednesdays? For in-stock items, aim to ship orders within one to five days. If you're selling perishables, you may want to have a policy that orders are sent out via overnight or second-day air at the beginning of the week (so your customers' brownies don't sit at a shipping warehouse over the weekend). But keep in mind that, in general, the sooner customers receive their items, the happier they will be.

Exchange. If an item is defective or the wrong size, a customer will likely request to exchange it. Make sure your policy directs customers to seek approval first and return the original item before a replacement will be sent out. While you may lose some revenue (either through the shipping cost or the loss of the defective product), at least you won't have to return the full revenue from the sale.

Return. If a customer wants to return an item, you can provide either a full refund or store credit. In either case, customers are usually responsible for the shipping charges to return the item. Offering complete refunds will make you a trustworthy seller, but it does come with a cost. For example, if a $20 item is purchased and your merchant processor charges you 2 percent plus a $0.10 transaction fee, when the item is returned you will have to refund the full $20 to the customer *and* you'll lose that additional $0.50 from the merchant processing fees—and this can add up over time. You can mitigate these losses by including a restocking fee to process the return (anywhere from 5 to 20 percent of the total sale) in your return policy. You might choose to have an "all sales are final" policy (items are sold as-is), but know that many online shoppers would be hesitant to buy products that are sight unseen and nonreturnable.

CUSTOMER SERVICE

Customer service is the attention you give your customers or potential customers. Brick-and-mortar retailers have the benefit of being able to interact with customers face to face, but as an online retailer you must gain their trust through your customer service channels. How you define or practice this can often determine whether your shop merely survives or thrives. Your goal should be to give your customers positive experiences so they'll keep coming back. Operate your business in an unethical way or give poor customer service, and negative word of mouth can spread. So focus on giving stellar service and maintaining a good reputation. If you can't afford to spend money on professional public relations, good customer service can be part of a public relations strategy. To create a positive reputation with your customers, follow these guidelines:

No. 1 KNOW YOUR PRODUCTS

Giving good customer service starts with understanding your products well—being knowledgeable about the best way for customers to consume or use the products you offer. Being able to give detailed measurements on a hand-sewn baby carrier will show your expertise and attention to detail regarding every product you bring into your shop.

No. 2 ANSWER E-MAIL

Sadly, e-mail can be easy to ignore. If you are slow to reply to messages, people can lose interest in their order or be so irritated that they post a negative comment on your Facebook wall. Respond to e-mail swiftly—preferably within twenty-four hours. It's also okay to automate some of your communication, such as sending instant order notifications and tracking information for shipments via e-mail to keep your customers informed of their order status.

No. 3 BE RELIABLE

Reliability means only making promises you can keep. If you tell your customer you'll overnight the RSVP cards that were missing from his order, then do everything you can to get to the post office in time. Broken promises are annoying, so before you make one be sure you can follow through.

No. 4 HANDLE COMPLAINTS COMPASSIONATELY

Listen to all complaints and do what you can to make the situation right. Stay professional at all times and avoid getting into a heated disagreement. If you have an "all sales are final" policy, be willing to bend it if your customer is really upset. It's often not worth the fight, since retribution can come in the form of negative feedback. If you do receive a negative rating, see what you can do to change the customer's mind and resolve the problem. If you make a mistake, admit it, apologize sincerely, and make it up to your customer with a replacement product or some other perk.

No. 5 BE PERSONAL

Good service is about establishing a relationship with your customers. Keep your communications professional and don't be afraid to engage people on a more personal level. However, you don't want to be too personal, explaining that you couldn't ship their order because your daughter was home sick with the flu, for example.

NONCHALANT MOM

Online Shop, Kid's Clothing
Wakefield, Rhode Island

Carina Schott's shop-owner experience started at home—in her guest-house, to be exact. Drawing on her fashion know-how from working at Esprit for ten years as well as other labels, she started ordering kids' clothing and accessories from friends who were also designers. She began by filling her guesthouse-shop with design-savvy kids' wear that couldn't be found elsewhere and selling to friends and local customers. It was key for Carina to offer a personal shopping experience—a feeling that she would later cultivate in her online shop, NonchalantMom.com. Little did she know that it was one of the earliest independent online children's boutiques. More than just a shop that puts a premium on customer service, the business features a sense of community, which she has developed by providing tips and parenting ideas to her custom-ers. With an esteemed business, Carina has created the ultimate "non-chalant" lifestyle for herself and her family.

 What was your vision for your Nonchalant Mom site?

I really wanted it to be graphically interesting and convey a wholesome, fresh look. For me, this meant a message of modernity with clear, clean aesthetics. I also wanted to encourage unisex style where people could be open to their boys wearing pink or girls wearing overalls and graphic T-shirts. For customer experience, a certain amount of professionalism needs to be present, but it was important to me that customers felt like they were shopping with a trusted friend. This was a bit esoteric, in that they had to like my vibe and honesty. If you are going to get into an online boutique business it helps to make sure your customers know that you are giving them something good—good for them and the planet. It was also important for my customers to have an uncomplicated shopping experience that meant they could get right down to the purchase.

Q *Did you have a business plan or mission statement?*

I wrote a business plan and I went to the Small Business Administration and went about trying to raise money. My business plan was a book! I had spreadsheet after spreadsheet and used images to convey my vision. I would show it to prospective lenders and they would say, "This is the best one that I've ever seen." I didn't get any financing; however, I am pleased to say that I have since exceeded all of the expectations from my business plan and have written two more since.

Q *What has your experience been like in baby-and-kid retail? And how did you go about marketing your store?*

It's wonderful to do online retail in the baby and children's market. I almost don't want to tell anyone that secret because everybody is so wonderful! You have couples who've just had their first baby and they are coming to purchase their first "firsts." They're moms and, if they know that you're a mom, there's great camaraderie with everyone. This includes vendors who are also moms.

On the other hand, developing a customer base is more difficult. There were months in the beginning when I didn't have a single customer. Then my business was mentioned on Daily Candy in January 2005 and I wound up with two hundred orders. I remember thinking, "This is crazy," because I was running out of inventory. At that point I decided that I was going to have to deal with everybody like they were a friend by being up front and personally responding to them, "I don't have that color; how about this . . ." The blogosphere has been a great help to the shop. I'm friends with a little circle of bloggers, and we blog about each other a lot, which also helps. Being on Design*Sponge and Bloesem for my European customers was amazing. Social networking, like blogging, is so important because it builds your word of mouth and puts you in touch with people who have similar tastes or interests as you.

Where does your inspiration come from when you're searching for the clothing and goods to be sold on the site?

I started my business out of our guesthouse, ordering collections from friends who designed and had something wonderful to offer. It was important that they were not available online so that my selection was unique. Today, I choose things differently. I get a vast amount of cold calls from different designers, but most of my finds are from researching online or at the kid trade shows such as Playtime in New York and Paris. When you walk the shows you need to remember that just because it's beautiful doesn't mean it will translate well online. It's also important to establish relationships with the vendors and see if they are willing to work with you on special pricing or letting you know when new designs are coming out.

What are some of the challenges you face as an independent online retailer?

Customers are smart these days . . . they know what is quality, whether something is well-constructed or -priced. Service should always be on an online retailer's mind, because you don't get to see your customers face-to-face. I always try and leave a phone number so people can call and hear a human voice instead of just e-mail. Last, I think that with an online shop it's important to have a range: something in very low, medium, and high price brackets.

What is your work-family life like?

When we first started, it all happened in our guesthouse. I would set up a "store," and customers and friends would come by to shop. It was a blast! As a family, we are on top of each other but I love that. I know what my kids are doing at all times. I do a lot of multitasking and I also work late. Our kids are in school now so I can get a good amount of work done. My husband is a painter and my office overlooks his studio. During the school year my husband keeps a tight schedule: We trade off mornings, one of us gets up with the kids and makes breakfast and takes them to school. Then after school the other person takes over. We always eat dinner together, even if we have tight deadlines.

SHIPPING AND FULFILLMENT

The success of your online shop will become evident to everyone, including your neighbors, when boxes of orders start lining your entryway and you get daily visits from a UPS driver who collects the day's shipment. But all this begins with shipping your first order. Understandably, orders need to arrive at their destination in good condition, but this is often easier said than done. Even if you've shipped a package before, you should take careful notes. Both of us learned about the follies of shipping the hard way—getting irate calls from customers whose products had arrived damaged. Not only did we have to resend a brand-new product, but we also had to pay to expedite the replacement package. Ouch.

The first step in ensuring this doesn't happen to you is to get good packaging materials. In your home office, you'll need to have a flat surface to serve as your shipping area. Stock it with necessities like a scale to weigh shipments, high-quality boxes and mailers, packing peanuts, a kraft paper roll, and sturdy packaging tape. Because packaging materials can be costly, avoid purchasing from a nearby office supply store and buy them instead at bulk or wholesale cost from packaging companies or paper distributors (like Uline.com or Papermart.com).

Fragile products need extra care—use bubble wrap, or double box the item. When you place the object in the box, make sure it will not come into contact with any of the box's sides. Fill up every square inch of the box with packing materials to make it resistant to compression and to prevent the item from shifting. Enclose items made of fabric in plastic bags, just in case the box gets wet in transit. A good rule of thumb is to assume that your box will be subject to a variety of conditions—snow or a heat wave, rough treatment as it's tossed wildly from truck to truck, and being placed underneath heavier boxes before getting to its destination—so you must take every precaution to ensure an order arrives safely. Placing a "fragile" sticker on doesn't provide much insurance.

Before you seal the box, include a packing slip to help avoid disputes about the box's contents, and keep a photocopy for yourself. You can choose from popular shipping services like UPS, FedEx, and the U.S.

Postal Service—all of which allow you to print labels online. If you find yourself shipping orders nearly every day, you'll be glad to know that all these services offer pickup (for a fee) so you don't have to lug thirty boxes around each day. Before you send out any packages, double-check each recipient's address. If you put the wrong street number, the shipping company may charge you a fee to correct the mistake or return the box to you. Eventually, you are bound to run into shipping issues like broken or damaged items, incorrect deliveries, and mysteriously disappearing packages. It happens. If a package is damaged or lost in transit, you can file a claim with the shipping company.

Fulfilling orders can be time consuming. If it becomes so overwhelming that you're constantly behind on orders, look into fulfillment houses in your area to handle warehousing, packing, and distribution. Transferring this responsibility will not only relieve your home of inventory, but it will also allow you to focus on other areas of your business, such as sending out press kits and updating your Web site.

INVENTORY ANALYSIS

As a shop owner, you have to keep your finger on the pulse of store sales. Keeping track of inventory using Excel or, even better, automatically through your e-commerce platform is essential. You'll need to identify which items are selling quickly, so you can replenish them more often, as well as pay close attention to the slow movers. Before you kick those items to the curb completely, analyze why they aren't selling. Why is no one interested in them? How are they shown on the Web site? Perhaps the images are too dark or too small. Maybe you need to reshoot the photos with a background that offers a sense of the scale of the item. Also, consider technical glitches—maybe the "buy" button isn't working. If you're certain that the item is not doing well because it isn't the right match for your customers, consider selling that item off by marking it down and dropping it from your regular inventory. Keep a running list or journal of your best-selling items as well as your duds.

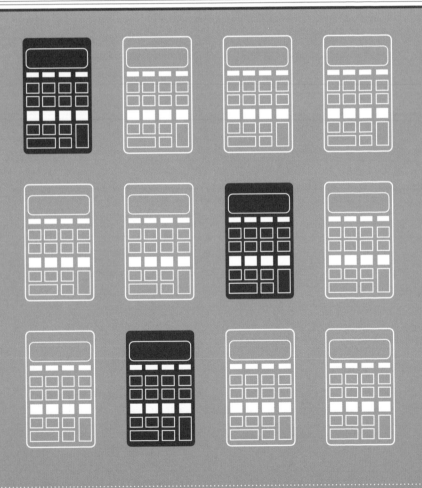

business
BASICS

chapter

06

By now, you probably have a good idea of what **BUSINESS YOU WANT TO PURSUE**. Although we've given you an overview and advice specific to executing blogging, freelancing, online retail, and product-based businesses, it's time to **REWIND AND START AT SQUARE ONE**. On the pages of this chapter you'll find instructions for **LAYING THE FOUNDATION** of your business, delving into finding the right name, financing, partnerships, and business plans.

ESTABLISHING AN ORIGINAL BRAND

Creating a brand is more than just figuring out a name and logo and slapping it on letterhead or a Web site. Think of your brand as a personality. The value of your brand comes from what your name and logo mean and the feelings that your business creates in people. For example, a person may purchase a Gucci bag because it connotes luxury and exclusivity. What feelings do you want people to have when they buy your line of

The value of your brand comes from what your name and logo mean and the feelings that your business creates in people.

children's clothing, visit your Etsy vintage store, read your design blog, or choose your illustration services? What words would customers use when describing your business? Write a list of key characteristics and clip some images from magazines that convey your brand's message. These emotions and word associations should help guide and define the look and feel of your brand.

Branding allows you to convey positive and intentional impressions of your company to your target market. It is more than just a part of your business—*it is your business*. Every detail connected to your business needs to be aligned with your brand—from the way you answer your business phone and handle customer service to the typeface on your Web site and the design of your banner ads. Analyze your competitors, and find a meaningful difference that will set your brand apart from others within your niche. Remember that your brand needs to express a unique point of view, style, and vision. It needs to be relevant to your target market and, above all, be memorable and recognizable.

When you've determined the brand or the personality of the company, consider these three major components to deliver your brand's message.

→ Design: Your logo, business card, letterhead, Web site, colors, typeface, and any graphics used to visually communicate the identity of your business

→ Communications and marketing: Your visual and verbal messages, including advertising, public relations, and any promotional tools used to attract clients, readers, or customers

→ Behavior: The manner in which you conduct your business— from your goals and mission statement to how you interact with followers over Twitter and respond to client inquiries

MISSION STATEMENT

To keep your business focused, you may find it helpful to draw up a mission statement. A verbalized belief system that articulates your goals, values, and vision, your mission statement defines what your business strives to be known for. It can be both specific and inspirational. Above all, it has to be something you believe in. Not only can it make you more motivated, but referring to it constantly will also make sure everything associated with your business is aiming in the same direction and toward the right purpose. It can help you determine which opportunities are right for your company. For example, if a mass-market company were to license your robot illustrations to appear on children's lunch boxes, folios, and pencils without your name—would that be in line with your mission? Remember that you can revisit and make changes to your mission as your company grows. Keep your mission statement front and center—literally posted somewhere in your work space—as a constant reminder of why you're here, what you're hoping to achieve, and how you're going to achieve it.

Sample Mission Statement

Green and Sweets:
A blog about eco-friendly design and organic confections.

➤ I will post about home décor products and fashion that are locally made and use eco-friendly materials or processes.

➤ I will post about confections that are locally made and use natural and organic ingredients and no artificial sweeteners or preservatives.

➤ I will create posts only about products I believe in.

➤ I will not post any advertorials, or posts sponsored by companies.

WHAT'S IN A NAME?

You toiled for nine months looking through baby names, eliminating the ones that were too popular or that your friends had already laid claim to, and negotiating with your hubby not to name the baby after his great-aunt Theodosia—and all that was for your *human* baby. So your *business* baby's name has got to be a piece of cake, right? Well, not quite.

One of the first considerations is to ask whether it is *you* or the *essence of your product* that you want to communicate through the business's name. "Chiu and Hartman Designs" delivers a different message than "Two Moms and a Kiln." If you are starting a service or freelance venture, it's natural to go eponymous, or name it after yourself. If clients are coming to you because of your signature flair for vintage-style photography, then using your name is a sensible option. If you want customers to be focused on the product or service itself, then coming up with a name that clearly enunciates that in a memorable and positive way is key.

We've met many entrepreneurial moms whose business names were inspired by their children or whose business name is rooted in a personal story. Incorporating something meaningful into the name is a great way to start your naming process, but be sure to also make the following considerations.

≫→ Write it out, say it aloud, and ask others to do the same. Was it hard for them to spell or pronounce? Did they think the name created a positive and appropriate association with the business?

≫→ Make sure it is distinct within your niche. If you're creating a baby product, you are well aware of the clever array of brands that have catchy, child-like phrases for names. You'll want to one-up them so it doesn't get lost in the sea of baby babble.

≫→ Remember that the name won't appear only on your business cards or product labels. It will also be your domain name, so visualize it as one long word with a ".com" (or other URL suffix attached). Envision how it would look on social media platforms like your blog, Facebook fan page, or Twitter.

≫→ Make sure the domain name has not been taken and that you can register for it. A domain registration service may tell you that the name with ".com" or ".net" is gone but that suffixes such as ".info" or ".biz" are available; you'll want to consider whether any of those will be practical for your brand's accessibility.

≫→ Make sure your company name hasn't been trademarked or service marked by checking with the U.S. Patent and Trademark Office. You may want to consider applying for legal protection, to prevent someone else from starting a company or selling a product with the same name. (See Trademarks and Service Marks, page 152.)

FINANCING YOUR BUSINESS

Without a doubt, starting a new business can become a financial strain on the family budget. It's normal for most small businesses to take a few years before they generate a steady income—which means there might be months when you do not receive any income at all. Putting your budget on paper will help your family to assess your finances and see what sacrifices need to be made while you're starting up. First, you need to make lists of your home and business expenses—the total amount is what you'll need each month in income to pay your bills each month. You'll have to check if you have enough money in savings or from your spouse's monthly income to cover these expenses for at least the first year. If you do not have enough, it means that you'll have to eliminate nonessential expenses like extended cable, a gym membership, or even your son's karate class, until your expenses are down to a manageable amount.

After putting together a budget sheet, you may decide that you do not have enough cash to get the business up and running. Loans are usually the first things to pop into your head when you think of how a small business can finance its start-up. The Small Business Administration (SBA) is a great way to check out the various types of guaranteed loans and grants that are available to you (visit www.sba.gov). They have a Small Business Planner section where you can find mentors as well as a search function to help you find the loans local to your area. Since stringent underwriting rules make traditional bank loans more difficult, microloans offered by nonprofit entities (listed at www.sba.gov) are some of the best types of loans for a small, creative business. You will still need to show a business plan and meet requirements, but they are known to be easier to secure than traditional bank loans.

Other types of loans you may consider, including ones that will affect your family finances, require some careful thought. Do you qualify for a home equity loan? Would it be wise to tap into your retirement funds? If you used credit cards to fund your start-up costs, could you repay them within a reasonable amount of time? Could you ask friends or family for a loan? If you do the latter, a legal contract or promissory note should always be written up, indicating whether it is secured or unsecured, what the payment schedule and interest is, and whether the loan provider becomes an investor in your company. Too often, personal relationships veil the seriousness of money matters, so putting it into writing can clarify any potentially hairy matters related to financial repayment and company involvement. Instead, you may want to consider getting friends and family to help fund your venture by putting your business plan on Kickstarter.com.

Outside of loans, there lies a world of possibilities for how you decide to financially plan (or bootstrap!) your business. Don't let the mentality of "If only I had more money" set you back. Think creatively and resourcefully about ways to maximize the dollars you do have. Since initial start-up costs have a way of snowballing, consider the following tips to seize control of them and keep your business running lean from the start.

No. 1 DON'T QUIT YOUR DAY JOB (JUST YET)

For many, the first big financial decision is deciding whether to keep that day job or whether the family can manage with the possibility of little or no income initially from your end, as well as added day-care costs. If you can slow the transition into full-time self-employment, it will help to ease the risk and avoid any dramatic loss in income for the family.

No. 2 ESTABLISH VENDOR CREDIT LINES

Do your best to establish credit with your top suppliers (such as the paper mill, or your yarn and wool supplier) and even any office supply vendors. This will allow you to defer payment, usually anywhere from fifteen to ninety days. In order to qualify, you may have to submit to a credit check and provide references.

No. 3 THINK GREEN

The phrase "reduce, reuse, recycle" can mean savings for your company. For starters, use some of your existing household furniture for your work environment, power down with energy-efficient lighting in your office, and print any draft documents on the reverse side of previous printouts. When possible, go paperless: Use e-mail fax services instead of receiving paper faxes, and pay your bills online.

No. 4 PRIORITIZE YOUR FINANCES

In the beginning, you may not have enough money to buy everything you need for your business. For example, rather than spend enormous outgo on fancy marketing collateral, downgrade your printing needs and direct more of your budget toward child care. Knowing that your kids are happy and well cared for while you get a dedicated chunk of uninterrupted work done trumps having letter-pressed business cards and stationery. Marketing collateral is important, but find less-expensive alternatives for your business needs when you can.

No. 5 TRADE FOR THE THINGS YOU NEED

The creative industry operates similarly to the beloved mom community, where you traded your rainforest play mat for a set of wood blocks—that is, you can barter for things you need. We regularly do this with other colleagues: We might design logos in exchange for catalog shots from a photographer or give up the name of a printing vendor in exchange for advice on Web site coding. Think about your talents and resources that could be exchanged for things you need in your business.

PETIT COLLAGE

Children's Home Décor
San Francisco, California

As a baby shower gift for her friend Sara, Lorena Siminovich, using her paper collection, made a collage of an owl family. It was something that she quickly put together before heading out the door, but that simple gesture was her lightbulb moment—from there she knew she wanted to make more of them and turn them into a business. Although that moment was accidental and serendipitous, much of Lorena's success with her business lies in her driven nature. With an "ask, ask, ask" philosophy, she's all about probing people and seeing what unfolds. With the knowledge she's extracted, she's scored sixteen book-illustration deals, six of which she's also written, four illustration-licensing deals from companies like our publisher, Chronicle Books, and even hard-to-get financing from the City of San Francisco. And in 2010, she added another feather to her cap: winning the Make Mine a Million $ Business competition, a national business competition for women entrepreneurs, which was founded by Count Me In for Women's Economic Independence and sponsored by American Express OPEN. It's clear that this is just the beginning and the best is yet to come for Petit Collage.

Q *How did you get started making collages?*

In 2006, I moved with my husband, Esteban, from New York to San Francisco, but I kept my job. I was telecommuting as the creative director for a gift company in New York. I had been working way too much on the computer and I was thirsty for interaction with real materials. I had always been a paper collector, so when my friend had a baby shower in 2007, I made a collage of an owl family on paper right before going out the door. I was so happy with making it and with the results that I couldn't sleep all night. I started to research materials and thought about putting the collage on wood. On a work trip to New York, I brought some collages mounted on wood to two boutiques. I just showed up at their shop—it was a risky, silly move. But luckily, the first store placed an order. However, I didn't have a price—so she told me what price it should be. Then I showed up at the next shop and told them that the first shop placed an order, and so they ordered on the spot as well.

Did you work from home when you first started? How soon did you hire help?

Yes, I worked from home, but for less than a year. Even though we owned a two-bedroom home, I don't function well work-wise from home. At the time, I was simultaneously easing out of my job as a creative director—I had reduced my role to only consulting for them—developing my illustration career, and launching the Petit Collage business. There was so much going on that I needed an assistant and my own studio space. I hired Annie, who started as my assistant and is now senior designer! Some people don't always function well with help, but I do.

How did you get your first book deal, illustration gigs, and licensing deals?

After leaving the gift company in New York, I continued to do freelance illustration work for them. And when I worked for them, I had made some contacts. I had gone to book fairs, like Book Expo America, for work and made contacts in the licensing departments of publishing houses. I just asked one of my contacts at a publishing house if they could tell me who I could talk to about doing a book. From my asking, I got a book deal to write and illustrate *Alex and Lulu: Two of a Kind* in 2009. But from all my asking and pitching around, I now have illustrated sixteen books, six of which I wrote, licensing deals with companies like MudPuppy, and even commission work from Pottery Barn. These days, people tend to find me; I think Citibank found me through a Google search! But I still prefer to be more proactive than reactive with getting jobs.

Have you been knocked off? How did you deal with that, in both a business sense and a mental sense?

Yes, I have been—people have done things very similar or nearly identical to mine. And I have sent a few cease-and-desist letters. I'm very proactive about getting all my work copyrighted by the U.S. Copyright Office. In the beginning, the copying really bothered me so much that I was upset and it became the center of my life for days. These days, there are copycats all the time and I have to laugh at some of it. I have to pick my battles; if I see anything at all that bothers me, especially by a bigger company, I will call my lawyer to discuss. I just try not to worry too much.

You gave birth to Matilda in 2009. How has having her changed how you view your business? Has she influenced any products in your line?

Radically. It's made the business more serious. I think, "If I'm not going to be home with my child, I had better do something really good." This business has to pay bills. I have to make this work. No more fooling around; otherwise I should just stay home with her. When she was born, I made thank-you notes that included an illustration of a little girl that I called Pinwheel Girl. That illustration was a "wish" for my daughter. People liked the illustration so much that I've since turned Pinwheel Girl into prints for my business. Also, when I first delivered Matilda, I was so inspired by the support I got in those rough first weeks from midwives, neighbors, and friends—that I made an illustration of a town, a community. It's called *It Takes a Village*, and it's also become one of the prints that I sell.

How do you finance your business?

In the beginning, I didn't need to finance my business because I didn't have to store inventory. I was making everything to order. Now I have more SKUs, or units. With product companies, you need a lot of capital to float the inventory, and you're constantly reinvesting in your company. There were months when I wouldn't take home salary. But about a year ago, I went to the Renaissance Entrepreneurship Center in San Francisco and they connected me with an organization that lends money on behalf of the city's government. But it's very competitive and they only fund a certain number of companies every year. It was really hard to qualify—I mean, I've bought three houses in my life and this was more difficult! But I'm stubborn and they gave me a loan for $25,000 at a very low interest rate. And recently, I did more research and met this man who works for a small bank that supports sustainable companies. I was able to get a nice line of credit at a great interest rate from them as well—and all this money goes to fund operations and inventory.

 You are a financing whiz! And in 2010, you were one of ten women business owners who won a national competition called Make Mine a Million $ Business. Congratulations! What's that experience been like?

It's changed my life. It's run by an amazing nonprofit called Count Me In for Women's Economic Independence. There's a statistic that out of ten million women-owned businesses, only 3 percent ever reach $1 million in revenue. Count Me In's goal is to have one thousand women entrepreneurs reach a million dollars in business revenue. Every year they put on this national competition and select ten businesses. Since the program began in 2005, roughly 30 percent of the women who have won the competition reached the million-dollar mark, and this is much higher than the national average of 3 percent. When I entered, more than two hundred companies entered the competition. I was one of twenty finalists that had to give a three-minute speech in front of an audience and a panel of expert judges. I became one of the ten winners! There are so many perks involved with this program—national publicity, business coaching, an American Express card (with credit), and much more! I feel much better knowing that I am an active member of a female entrepreneurial community and, even better, a sisterhood of women trying to do the same thing. We even have a Yahoo! group where we provide support and tips to each other.

BUSINESS ESSENTIALS

As soon as you begin offering your products or services for profit or selling ads on your blog, you are considered a business—and, therefore, are subject to taxes, rules, laws, and regulations concerning it. Following are the basic necessities for making your business official.

Legal Structure

Your choice of legal structure determines more than just taxes. Making the right choice ensures that you are able to grow the business financially in the ways you see fit while protecting your family's assets (in case you are sued). Some solo small-business owners may choose sole proprietorship, while partners may go for a general partnership. However, if tax and asset protection are high on your list of concerns, you may want to consider other legal structures such as a limited partnership, limited liability company, S-Corporation, or C-Corporation. Filing processes and fees vary for each one, so consult an accountant or lawyer to see which structure is best for you.

Business License

You need to apply for local, state, or federal licenses depending on the type of business you are running. If you are selling handmade jewelry you may only need to register for a city license, while a makeup artist may need to obtain a state license. You can check requirements by contacting your secretary of state or by visiting www.sba.gov, which offers information on license requirements. In addition, the site provides information and applications based on your zip code and location.

Federal Tax ID

If you are a sole proprietor without employees, it's not necessary to apply for a federal tax ID; your social security number (SSN) will suffice in tax documents. If you have another legal structure, have employees, or simply don't feel comfortable giving your SSN to vendors or clients, you should apply for a federal tax ID, also known as an Employer Identification Number (EIN), through the IRS. You can do this free online by visiting www.irs.gov.

Fictitious Business Name

Your state law requires you to file for a fictitious name statement, known as "Doing Business As" (DBA), if you are using a business name other than your own name. First, you'll want to check that the name has not been registered by someone else. From there, you'll apply at your local county clerk's office or at the secretary of state. Depending on where you live you may also need to publish a notice in your local newspaper.

Seller's Permit

If you plan on selling or reselling a product for profit and your state collects sales tax, you will need to obtain a seller's permit in order to purchase or sell those goods. Sometimes referred to as a "resale license" or "sales tax license," this permit is usually issued by a state agency, like your state's department of revenue. You'll need to have your business license and federal tax ID handy when you apply. Once it's issued, keep this certificate accessible so that you can attend trade shows and make purchases with a wholesaler.

Zoning

Your city's zoning department or chamber of commerce can determine whether you can operate your business in your location. Although communities have been more accepting of the growing trend of home-based businesses, you may want to check with your residential board, which may have limitations such as noise regulation rules (especially if your business engages in a particularly noisy craft like woodworking).

Business Bank Account

You will need to open a dedicated business checking account and apply for a separate credit card for all of your business transactions. Your business and personal transactions should not be commingled. It's also a good idea to open a business savings account as well to deposit a portion of your income in case you have to pay quarterly taxes.

Insurance

If you plan to work from home, check with your homeowner's insurance carrier to see if you have adequate coverage. It is in your best interest to make sure you are fully protected. Factors such as equipment, daily foot traffic, or employees may affect this coverage and can be added on in a "rider" to your policy. If your business involves visits from clients, customers, or employees, look into coverage for injury liability and worker's compensation insurance.

Health Insurance

Having health insurance is a must, especially if you are not covered by your spouse's policy. In fact, that is one of the benefits of your nine-to-five job that you'll miss, and it might startle you not to have that as a given when you are starting out on your own. Although it might be tempting to skip paying those premiums and just wing it, this is a category you don't want to skimp on. These days, there are numerous health coverage plans that serve a variety of budgets and needs. If you are leaving your job, you can continue your health insurance for a period of time with Consolidated Omnibus Budget Reconciliation Act (COBRA) benefits. If you want minimum coverage, consider a medical plan that will help take care of hospital and surgery costs (though you'll pay the rest out of pocket). Take advantage of group insurance rates through affiliations such as non-profits and artists' guilds through which rates are lowered because of the purchasing power of a combined group. If you have a local mommy group or a group of friends with their own businesses, you can even create your own group health plan. And don't forget to check out the Internet for sites that provide side-by-side data on costs, benefits, options, or limitations for different companies.

When you start something new and daunting like a business, it's tempting to want a partner—someone to lean on or share the ups and downs with. We certainly entertained this idea heavily, moving through the Rolodex of cousins, old college friends, or coworkers with whom we had bonded throughout the years and knew we could count on. But loyalty in kin and friendship is only a fraction of what it takes to have a successful partnership. Partners should complement, not replicate, one another. While having a partner can allow you to split up the work it takes to hit goals, a mismatched team with different expectations can slow or even halt the growth of your business. Can you both be in sync when it comes to decision making on all fronts—both macro and micro levels, aesthetic and branding issues, and organizational and communicative details? It is also important for partners to have key strengths or talents that they call their own not only for the sake of the business but to also gain a sense of independence within it. So before making a commitment, you might find it valuable to try a small project or even take a trip together to get a feel for how you will work as partners.

Whether you choose your best friend or a colleague, an important next step is to draw up a partnership agreement with the help of a lawyer or accountant. How will you divide the business—50/50, 60/40, or some other percentage split? (For two partners, having at least a 49/51 arrangement is helpful so that one person has the ultimate say in stalemate situations.) What is your exit clause or contingency plan should you or your partner opt out of the business? A good portion of the agreement should be dedicated to spelling out your roles in detail. This means everything from how each of you will fulfill operations of the business and how much time is expected to how you communicate with and report to one another on a daily, weekly, and monthly basis.

FAMILY AFFAIR

If you're considering partnering with your spouse, know that being a couple in business together has advantages (you have complete trust in each other) and disadvantages (any stress from your business may affect your personal life). Financial matters can be a particularly sore spot. Even if you are *the* dynamic duo, you might find that one of the biggest challenges is to figure out how not to be in business mode around the clock. If your pillow talk starts to focus on shipping out packages, it might be good to assign a curfew for shop talk. Furthermore, if you work from your home, it may feel like everything is swirling together—meetings, marketing calls, kids' activities, and grocery shopping can become one gigantic blur. Delineate and define your time as partners versus parents, so that you don't feel overwhelmed. On the plus side, you'll be spending more time together than you did when you were working in separate jobs. While not every couple is meant to partner in business, a successful team can have a unified vision for the betterment of each other and their family.

PROTECTING YOUR WORK

We like to think that our industries (stationery and print) are among the most convivial and good natured. However, they are also subject to the downsides of competition and unfair practices—namely, copying. Creative work can be a gray area when it comes to what is protected and what is not, so brushing up on rules about copyright, trademarks, and patents is helpful. In our experience, protecting yourself against infringement is one of the best proactive measures you can take.

Copyright

You may not realize that once you sketch a woodland scene onto a note card, it becomes copyrighted. A copyright gives you, and *only you*, the right to copy, distribute, and create derivatives of your original work. It protects original works such as artwork or designs, novels, songs, and architecture. Fashion, however, cannot be copyrighted because it is considered a utilitarian and necessary article. Although registration with the U.S. Copyright Office is voluntary, if you ever need to take someone to court you will need to register, so it's advisable to have it done at the beginning. Also, if registration is made within three months after creation, it lengthens the copyright owner's statutory damages in court actions. Often simply showing that you have a registered copyright can scare a copycat, saving you from taking any potential legal action. The application process is straightforward and can be filed online at the U.S. Copyright Office (www.copyright.gov). In addition to registration information, the site has a detailed list of frequently asked questions, such as "How do you protect my recipe?" as well as a list of countries where your work may not be protected should you go international.

Patents

There are patents that protect either an invention or a discovery. A utility patent protects a new and useful method or process (a spill-proof cup, for example), while a design patent protects the "ornamental" appearance of an invention (computer icons fall into this category). Visiting the U.S. Patent and Trademark Office Web site (www.uspto.gov) will help you determine which kind of patent is most appropriate and how to file for it. Additionally, if you and your little one have invented something together, check out the special rules and considerations in the USPTO's section dedicated specifically for young inventors.

Trademarks and Service Marks

The terms *trademark* or *service mark* refer to the unique logo, sign, or brand indicators that a company or producer uses to establish the unique origin of their goods or services. As a new business, you want your name to stand out in the marketplace (whether that's your neighborhood or the global village of the Internet). To protect your business name and identity, file for a trademark for your business name (if your business is a service one, then you'll need a service mark). Visit the U.S. Patent and Trademark Office Web site (www.uspto.gov) for registration information. One of the first steps will involve conducting a search to see if the business name you want to trademark or service mark is currently being used by someone else.

Creative Commons

Creative Commons, a nonprofit organization in San Francisco, California, has also created an alternative to the "all rights reserved" copyright, called a Creative Commons license. They've created six different "flexible" copyright licenses that allow you, the designer, to determine what rights you reserve and what rights you waive for the creative common good. For example, an "Attribution" license (which is the most accommodating license) for your photograph will allow people to take your work and distribute, copy, sell, or perform it, as long as they credit you. Creative Commons provides you with symbols associated with each type of license to place on your Web site that communicate how you would like to share your intellectual property. Since the organization began in 2001, millions of licenses have been created and they are all free of charge.

RECORD KEEPING

Now that you're in business, any payments or charges you accrue solely for business purposes (meals with clients, parking fees, or books for research) are considered tax-deductible expenses. That means the lunch you had with your accountant can be considered an expense, but dinner with your mother for her birthday is not. Any expenses that could be personal require additional proof of their business nature—so for business meals, write on the receipt the name of the person you were with and the nature of the meeting. File your receipts right away as well—don't let it get lost with all the other tchotchkes that tend to accumulate in a mother's bag.

In addition to maintaining receipts, make sure you manage your business's books carefully. You can record your income and expenses by hand with preformatted ledgers or through programs such as Excel, Peachtree, and QuickBooks. There are also many free online programs that will not only help you manage your books but also provide you with graphs, spending pie charts, and saving calculators. You should find a system that captures your bookkeeping records and bank information, manages your tax filings like your state's sales tax, and produces commonly used forms like purchase orders or invoices. If you can't tell your payables from your receivables, consider hiring a bookkeeper or an accountant to manage your finances. Giving up this responsibility can free up time to work on other aspects of your business—not to mention reducing any paperwork headaches.

ESTABLISHING A HOME OFFICE

The financial benefits of an at-home office are obvious: You save on rent, utilities, and other expenses. Keep in mind that the space you choose should be your official haven, hopefully away from little prying hands and attention-hungry pets—spare bedrooms, garages, and basements are often good nominees. You can also write off office space as well as the costs for operating it (phone line, supplies, equipment), but only if your work space is used exclusively and regularly for business. If your basement office doubles as a playroom, it won't be tax deductible.

For a mother, flexibility is key with everything, including defining your "work space." Inevitably, it will migrate with you wherever you go. There may be days when you sort through invoices on the dining table as your children complete their homework. You may have to take calls under the stairwell or in a closet so that your napping infant doesn't hear you. The trusty old car during dance rehearsal may not be the most glamorous place to work, but take solace in the fact that almost every mom entrepreneur has had to work under these conditions in order to balance work and family schedules.

ONLINE TOOLS OF THE TRADE

The digital age has allowed us to run at lightning speed—that is, if we can remember our twenty or so login names and passwords! Nevertheless, the Internet is vital for organizational tools and online communication to assist small creative businesses. The following are some tools and tips to consider.

- Inspiration gathering tools, like Evernote, can help you to capture and organize all of those bright shiny ideas that keep flashing before your eyes. If you're looking for some inspiration from others who share your love for antique lace, check out Pinterest.

- Online calendars are a mom's best friend. A good one allows other members of the family or staff to sign in and sends reminder e-mails or texts to your phone. Some of our favorites are from Google, Yahoo!, and Cozi.

- Take advantage of free online document systems (such as Google Docs). It's a great way to share files that others can view and download.

- Get access from remote computers. Services like LogMeIn (www.logmein.com) allow you to access your home computer from even your mobile device.

- Consider buying groceries or household goods online. For example, having diapers delivered can shave off hours that you can dedicate to work!

READY, SET . . . GOAL

Being a work-at-home mom means maximizing every window of time we can get. Despite the best of intentions, precious work time is often misspent. Setting goals within a set period are what get the wheels of your business turning—and actually accomplishing them will keep you happy. The following are some ways to help you create goals, organize them, and help you reach the satisfying feeling of completion.

➤➤ Interview yourself: Where do you see your food blog in a month, six months, or a year—and what will you need to do to leave your day job? Jot down these answers to set your long-term goals—and make sure that your goals and timeline are realistic.

➤➤ Subdivide: It's much easier to break down the steps leading to the big task and see it in phases. Planning for a trade show booth can be daunting—but if you make a list of things to accomplish (electrical, shipping and drayage, design, etc.), you can further break those tasks down into smaller biweekly goals.

➤➤ Plan ahead and balance: Every evening write a list of goals you'd like to accomplish for the next day. (You'll find that it's easier to start your day with this list in hand.) You should also organize your to-do's in order of urgency or difficulty—and be sure to include both easy and hard goals.

BUSINESS PLAN

In each of our businesses, we have to admit that we never had an "official" business plan. But we took copious notes, wrote mission statements, sketched product designs far into the night, and talked to people about our hopes and expectations. Formalized or not, it was essential to give ourselves a trajectory (however creatively recorded) and points of focus in order to reach each milestone. Our businesses began before we had children and, now that we both have families and even busier lives, we shudder to think of moving forward with any new aspect of our business without at least a mission statement that has pared down our priorities and a list of goals.

Unless you are approaching a traditional banking institution for a loan, starting a business does not require a fifty-page business plan. If you are making one for only your eyes to view, whether it is fashioned as an abstract dream board or written up as a formal document, the important thing is to be clear about your vision and goals. Your business plan is your blueprint for action—a scheme showing how to get you where you want to go. It should be your guide in the months and years ahead. The following are some essentials in your business plan.

- Basic information on your company, including the business name, location, partners and roles, legal structure, and a brief summary or description

- Your mission statement

- A timeline that captures snapshots of your business as you envision it in six months, one year, five years, and beyond

- Audience and marketplace: profiles of your target readers, customers, or clients

- Marketing strategy for print, online, local outreach, and word-of-mouth campaigns

- Description of goods, services, or content offered (as well as any production or editorial schedules)

- Financial plan and revenue projections

- Exit plan: Do you plan to sell the business or stay on as an adviser?

getting
THE WORD OUT

Now that you know that you want to start a blog about your culinary pursuits, or an Etsy shop hawking your handmade lotions— it won't be much good if no one knows that it exists. How will you get people to **FOCUS THEIR ATTENTION ON YOU?** Through marketing! Marketing involves everything you do to **GET YOUR BUSINESS ON THE RADAR**—from sharing your blog with a fellow mom in your child's play group to placing an advertisement in your local paper. While marketing might seem like another expenditure tugging at your checkbook, it's more than just an expense—**IT'S AN INVESTMENT.** A good marketing plan will **BUILD YOUR BUSINESS**; without one, you won't have anything to drive people to your site. So take note of all the tactics you might use, including networking both online and offline, publicity, and advertising, to **DEVELOP A MARKETING PROGRAM** that distinguishes your business from the others and sends your business skyward.

BUSINESS CARDS

Business cards may be small, but don't underestimate their ability to make a big impression. In fact, Meg collects business cards for both information and inspiration. Indeed, business cards can speak about your brand and boast of your creativity. A well-designed card not only shares your contact information but also heightens interest in what you do. It represents you when you're not there—nudging the holder to go to your

 A well-designed card not only shares your contact information but also heightens interest in what you do.

site to learn more about you. When you design yours, try not to clutter the card with too many design elements or information, like your Facebook page and Twitter handle. The basics—your e-mail, phone number, and Web site—should suffice. Be sure to print a bunch, carry them with you at all times, and get in the habit of handing them out like they're Halloween candy.

PRINT COLLATERAL

Letterhead, mailing labels, invoices—oh my! Business cards are just the tip of the iceberg when it comes to the business materials that are available to you. While letterhead and other stationery may make your business seem more legit, you should only get these items if you generate a lot of paper correspondence or do a lot of shipping. For example, letterhead may be necessary for a design consulting agency, but not if you have a blog as a business. There are also other types of print collateral that may assist with marketing your business—brochures are helpful if you have a multitude of baby food flavors to offer, and postcards show-casing your photography are good leave-behinds when meeting with a client. Since material is difficult to change once it's been printed (we've all seen restaurant menus with embarrassing typos), make sure you ask friends and peers to review your design and your copy to make sure the layout is professional and the text doesn't contain any spelling errors or incoherent language.

SPREADING THE GOOD WORD

If you're doing innovative, creative work and providing over-the-top cus-tomer service, then there's a good chance your clients are talking up your business. Word-of-mouth advertising happens when people spontaneously tell their friends, colleagues, or family about your business because they had a great experience working with you. They felt so good about

 Word-of-mouth advertising happens when people spontaneously tell their friends, colleagues, or family about your business because they had a great experience working with you.

what you're doing that they were compelled to tell others. Think of it as "business karma"—do good (make great things or treat people with care and attention) and good things will come to you, in the form of sales, clients, or an increased readership. While word of mouth is a tactic that should be in everyone's marketing plan, you shouldn't rely on it alone. Word-of-mouth outreach falls into the category of "hope marketing"—you have no control over it; you can merely hope people are out in the wild acting as spokespersons for your business.

CYNTHIA ROWLEY

Fashion Design
New York, New York

The funny thing about getting your "big break" is that you never know when that day will come. Certainly, Cynthia Rowley—back when she was a fashion design student at the Art Institute of Chicago—had no idea that wearing one of her creations on the train would catch the eye of a major New York department store buyer. That serendipitous event led Cynthia to create and sell her first collection before graduation day. More than twenty years, sixty eponymous shops, numerous awards, and scads of press mentions later, she's proven that she's got staying power and that her talents don't lie in women's fashion alone. Cynthia has authored several books, including *Slim: A Fantasy Memoir* and the hugely popular *Swell* lifestyle book series with Ilene Rosenzweig. She's applied her design eye to menswear, eyewear, handbags, shoes, umbrellas, and even a signature fragrance. She's partnered with companies like Target to create a home décor line, Roxy for a surf apparel line, and, most recent, Babies"R"Us for a children's clothing line. (By the time you read this, she will probably have added another talent or two to her repertoire.) But of her many jobs, the one she considers most important is mother to her daughters, Kit and Gigi.

Can you describe the early days of your business when you launched your first collection? What were the biggest lessons you learned in those early years?

I don't know if those early days can even be described! I was that typical "girl from a small town with a big dream." I was so naive at the beginning, and it really helped me believe that anything was possible. I still believe that, actually!

My career really started when a buyer at a very prestigious department store spotted me in a self-made jacket on the El train during my time at the Art Institute of Chicago. I met with her on a Friday afternoon and sewed all weekend to meet her Monday morning deadline. Style numbers one through five of the Cynthia Rowley Collection—three dresses, a tricked-out velveteen jacket, and a matching shirt-jacket and pant ensemble—were born from that experience. I'm still not totally sure what people were drawn to initially in my work, as I have always just designed clothes that I myself would want to wear. But whatever it was, that first order of a dozen velveteen jackets sold out in record time.

As far as the lessons I've learned, I think I'm still learning them: Never take "no" for an answer; be grateful for what you have; hard work always pays off. As cliché as these expressions are, they're so important when you're starting out. I think one of the most important lessons that I'm still trying to learn is to balance, whether it's between art and commerce within my designs, or between home and work in my life as a whole. It's all about balance.

 What are some of the things you do to balance work and family life?

My older daughter, Kit, often comes to sit and draw in my office after school, and I think she really loves the environment. Gigi, my younger daughter, will pop in with my husband, Bill, to say hi pretty regularly, too. I'm really lucky to have them close by. I think there's a fluidity between personal life and work for me that maybe doesn't exist for every designer or career person. But for me, it's just the natural order of things.

 You are such a multidisciplinary creative! What is your design process like?

Ever changing. I don't believe in the boundaries of design, because inspiration can come from anywhere at any time. As a mom, I think it's important to retain your wide-eyed wonderment at the world around you so that you can communicate that energy to your kids. I still have the same childlike willingness to explore and create as I did when I was a little girl.

How has collaborating with brands like Roxy and Target enriched you as a designer?

I only pursue collaborations that resonate with me personally. As my husband says, I've been "trying to surf" for ten years, so my interest in working with Roxy evolved from what I saw as a void in the market: There were no well-designed wetsuits that also complemented the female body. The Target collaboration was incredible because I was an early pioneer of that high-low dynamic that is now so commonplace. I've always believed that that's how people shop: They look for added value through great design. With Hooray By Cynthia Rowley, my collection at Babies"R"Us, I wanted to work within this same logic. Moms should be able to find children's clothes that are thoughtful, fun, *and* accessible. Obviously, once I became a mom, this particular category of fashion became even more relevant to me.

Looking back over the years, is there an accomplishment that you are most proud of?

Every day is a new challenge, with new obstacles and celebrations, and I'm proud of getting through every one of those days as best I could.

INTRODUCE YOURSELF

Being an active agent of your work means letting people know what you do—whether it's in subtle ways, like wearing your felted floral pin about town, or in more active ways, like attending a conference to network with other bloggers. Either way, you're basically attempting to trigger an opportunity to speak about your work. But don't let self-interest be your only motivator, looking at people as if they're walking bank accounts. Networking is about developing relationships. You should show a genuine interest in other people as well as in subjects beyond your expertise. Use this Ralph Waldo Emerson quote as your guide: "Every man I meet is in some way my superior, and I can learn of him." That means that if you're a good listener you can learn something to help your business progress.

 You should show a genuine interest in other people as well as in subjects beyond your expertise.

Everyone has a unique story and perspective; maybe the person you're speaking with used to be a copywriter at an ad agency—that could be helpful for your business!

You also need to adopt a likable persona, which means refraining from complaining or whining about the food at the conference to someone you just met. If you make a genuine connection with someone and present your optimistic side, they're more likely to remember you and be interested in helping you out. And the more people you meet and make a positive impression upon, the easier it will be for you to make connections to vendors, press, and clients as your business grows.

NICE TO MEET YOUR AVATAR

When Meg started her first business (an online wedding shop) in 1999, she had to attend local holiday fairs to meet other creative peers or e-mail other creative-business owners in the hopes of sparking a friendship. Nowadays, connecting with your peers and even your market can happen faster and easier than ever—and you can do it without ever meeting in person. Without a doubt, social media has had a profound effect on how small businesses promote themselves. Namely, it's given us the technology to deepen the relationships we have with our peers, clients, and fans.

Blogs

Although we discussed how to make blogging your business in chapter 2, blogs can also be a strong self-promotional tool for any kind of business. Blogging allows you to show a more personal side to your business—you can use it to share your interests and aesthetic in other realms outside

Blogging allows you to show a more personal side to your business—you can use it to share your interests and aesthetic in other realms outside of work.

of work. Since it's written in a much more informal voice, visitors feel like they're getting to know you better. With her blog, Cat has been able to show behind-the-scenes shots of the trade shows she's participated in, helping to enrich her readers' understanding of her business. You can also post in-progress shots of your latest film project, for example, to test out new ideas, receive feedback, and begin to generate a buzz. It can also be a medium to highlight your success stories, such as a recent press mention in the *Wall Street Journal* or an award you've received in a

DIY screen-print contest. Blogs can even lead to book deals—publishers can see your writing style and gauge your expertise in a subject, and of course they may also like your readership numbers, since they may represent future sales for the book.

Facebook

Friend networks such as Facebook bring together a captive audience who will undoubtedly be interested in supporting you. Such a network can help you renew old friendships as well as maintain new ones with very little effort or cost. You might instantly gain thirty "friends" from the moms in your son's play group, a hundred of your friends from high school and college, and yet another hundred from friends of friends. If you can balance both, open a personal page and a business fan page that links back to your Web site. It's good to have both, so that you can keep the general masses (clients, blog readers, fans) from seeing any potentially private or less-than-professional images posted to your profile, like your high school senior portrait or your girls' night out two days ago. If you worry that your business fan page is yet another thing begging for new content and your attention, the good news is that you can use Facebook or a social media dashboard to aggregate your other social media content. You can directly link to the posts on your blog and use your tweets as Facebook status messages, reducing the amount of new content and messages you need to produce for each outlet.

Twitter

Twitter is simple: It's a free service that lets anyone send 140-character messages answering the question "What's happening?" That message, called a "tweet," can be sent from your computer or thumb-typed onto your smartphone and will be seen by your "followers." While it doesn't sound like much, it's a powerful communication tool for networking and even finding out information. For Meg, it's facilitated online friendships, and it once even helped her to find a hotel. In response to a tweet asking for a recommendation for an affordable hotel in New York, some of her Twitter peers pointed her toward a few hip, budget hotels—with links. That beats doing a Google search any day.

Truly, Twitter was made for moms. The 140-character parameter is a blessing in disguise for all the stop-and-go activities that happen in one day. You can tweet about recent press you've gotten, bits of your life, random thoughts in your mind, a rant about a television show, the weather—anything goes! The fact that its format is easy to access on your mobile phone makes it possible to chronicle things right as they happen. While your Facebook personal page facilitates interaction among a circle of friends, your "followers" on Twitter will likely be people you have never met or heard of before, but who share similar interests with you.

When you enter the Twitter world, you might feel like you've just landed in a foreign country. Words are truncated, symbols abound, and links are unrecognizable. Here's a quick cheat sheet that will help you assimilate into the culture.

@username: This is your Twitter handle and it should include all or part of your business name. Keep it short, since characters are so valuable in a tweet. When someone tweets to you or mentions you, that person will place your handle in their tweet and it will appear in your "mentions" feed.

Retweet: If you like a tweet that someone else posted—whether it was interesting, helpful, or just plain funny—you can click on "Retweet" and it will put the entire post into your followers' feeds.

RT: Short for "retweet," this abbreviation is used when you want to also insert a comment before the original tweet. For example, if @catseto tweets, "We're having a book signing at 7PM for Mom Inc. Meet us at my shop at 2406 Polk Street in SF!" you can retweet, "Can't wait to meet you both! RT @catseto We're having a book signing at 7PM for Mom Inc. Meet us at my shop at 2406 Polk Street in SF!"

Shortened URLs: Because of the brevity of each tweet, there isn't any room to place complete URLs. If you go to a URL-shortening site like T.co, Bit.ly, or Tiny URL, all you have to do is provide them with the permalink and, in exchange, you'll get a bite-size URL to place in your tweet. Some social media monitoring platforms, like HootSuite and TweetDeck, offer URL shortening as a part of their service.

 # (Hashtag): If you want to join a conversation or start one, you can use a hashtag, or the # symbol followed by a term or phrase indicating a topic. If you look on the "Trends" panel, you can see a few of the most popular topics being discussed. Click on a hashtag and you can see all the tweets that were made on that topic.

#FF ("FollowFriday"): On Fridays, users often share the handles of their favorite Tweeps (short for "Twitter" plus "peeps," or people who use Twitter) whom they follow.

Messages: You can send private messages (sometimes called "direct messages") to people who are following you. The reverse is also true: You can only receive a message from people whom you're following.

Now that you have the Twitter lingo down, you'll be ready to send your first tweet. Don't worry about carefully planning your tweet to pass it off as a seemingly off-the-cuff, clever missive. No one will notice or care how much work you put into crafting your tweet. Just don't think too much—type something simple like "I'm finally joining Twitter!" It doesn't matter if you love it or hate it—just type it. That tweet will be a fading memory and you can move on to your next tweet.

YOUR WEB SITE

Without a doubt, having a Web site is instrumental for any business. Every day, new advancements are made that will make it easier and faster for people to find you. Since fewer and fewer people are using the Yellow Pages, your Web site is how you'll provide most people with your contact information. In addition, your Web site is basically a high-tech version of your brochure, catalog, or portfolio—another extension of your brand. Web sites don't have to be expensive to look good; you can use templates on Cargo Collective or Wordpress to build your site. If you want something more customized, hire a graphic designer and programmer to put together a site for you. However you choose to make your site, it should look professional and creative, have easy navigation, open external links in a new window, utilize fonts that are easy to read, use common words rather than industry speak, and, above all, be updated frequently.

Site Analysis

Do you want to know who's visiting your site? If you have a blog, especially as a business, tracking statistics and compiling data will be critical. While there are many options, we take advantage of Google Analytics to do the heavy lifting of parsing our traffic data. Regardless, your analytics tools should give you a view into not only how many visitors your blog or Web site receives per day but also where that traffic is originating (both geography- and referral-wise, as in from other sites or through search engines). You'll also get to see how that traffic ebbs and flows. Reviewing this detailed feedback on a regular basis will help you to understand how quickly the public's awareness of your company or blog is growing, particularly if any ads you've placed are directing traffic to it.

BE YOUR OWN PUBLICIST

If you want to get press for your business, you need to think like a publicist—which means you need to be able to see media opportunities and angles in everything you do. However, you can't buy publicity; you can only take strides to make it happen. Foremost, publicity needs a good story—you need something worthwhile to crow about.

The good news is that news and editorial outlets as well as blogs are all hungry for content! Television news programs have to fill up a half-hour of programming, editors need to fill the pages of their newspaper or magazine with stories, and blogs need to post something daily. They are all desperate for a good story or something visually inspiring. You just need to figure out what your stories are and tell those stories to the right journalists, and if you do it well the media will flock to you and write about you. It's the angle that makes a story newsworthy. For example,

Meg hosts independent design sample sales called Modern Economy. It's an event held twice a year, so you can imagine how hard it would be to stir up press every single time. When she launched, the angle of her first press release focused on its newness; it was the "first ever sample sale of independent home designers" and the novelty of the idea got the

 If you want to get press for your business, you need to think like a publicist—which means you need to be able to see media opportunities and angles in everything you do.

event featured in several blogs. In subsequent sales, she had to be more creative and think about angles. Simply announcing that she was having yet another sale was hardly newsworthy. To promote one sale, she focused on the story behind starting the sale (she had a big surplus inventory of pillows and didn't know what to do with them)—it netted articles in *7x7* and *Sunset* magazines. For another sale, she considered the state of the economy and described the events in a press release as "sales that were helping independent designers through the recession"; that effort resulted in press from both the *San Francisco Chronicle* and the *New York Times*.

However, if you have a product-based business, angles are helpful but not always necessary if you're simply looking to get your charm necklace into the market section (an area showcasing latest goods) of a magazine or newspaper. If you can't formulate a story angle, you shouldn't send out a press release; rather, you'd include a product information sheet with your press kit.

Press Kit

A press kit is a package of materials assembled to help the media understand your business. There are two key features a press kit must have: It
should tell a clear story about the company and display some originality
in its presentation. That being said, it does not have to be an expensive
undertaking. What you lack in funds, you can make up in imagination.
You can even use materials from your own product; for instance, to
announce her new custom wedding collection, Cat created a press invitation based on the design of an existing invitation. However you choose to
present your business in a press kit, you should also have a digital version, or PDF, of it. Press kits generally contain the following items.

- A biography or company history with photographs

- Reprints of press mentions, including clippings from publications
  and screen shots of online publications

- A press release, if applicable

- A product information sheet, if you are promoting a specific item

- Sample products, if you can spare them

Media Mailing List

You'll need to gather information and put together a media mailing list,
which can include television, radio, print editorial, and blogs or online
magazines. Scope out news station Web sites and magazine mastheads
for the names of reporters or editors along with their e-mail addresses.
Consider which journalists are most appropriate to receive the press kit;
if you're promoting a local event, you'll probably want to contact local or
regional media first. There is also a code of exclusivity you need to follow;
you should contact publications or blogs with a single pitch one at a time
(starting with the media outlets you most want to get into) and move
on to the next media contact only after you've received a rejection (or
haven't received a reply within a couple weeks of your inquiry, depending

on how often the publication is printed). Of course, if the publications are noncompeting—for example, if you're pitching alpaca throw pillows to *Real Simple* and a burlap ring-bearer pillow to *Martha Stewart Weddings*— it's fine to contact them at the same time. Once you've made media contacts, you should nurture those relationships. If you continue to provide them with good stories, they'll be happy to give your business press. And if you grow to be an expert in your trade, you can offer to write up articles or provide guest editorial for them as well.

PRESS RELEASE NECESSITIES

- Place FOR IMMEDIATE RELEASE at the top of the document.

- Include contact information including a point person, phone number, and e-mail address.

- A bold headline should summarize the story (capitalize the first letter of every word in the headline except conjunctions, prepositions, and articles).

- Right before the first sentence, put the city and state as well as the date of the press release.

- Write the copy as if it were an article in a magazine (in third person). Editors will often lift copy directly from the release and place it into the article.

HIRING A PUBLICIST

Publicity can easily become a full-time job. Outsourcing it costs money, but it's an expense that can pay for itself. Publicists are often bubbly, well-spoken people who may be able to riff on your products better than you could. They have a unique talent for thinking up story angles and pitches you might have not considered, as well as a knack for conceptualizing attention-getting press kits. They're also whizzes at writing press releases, using persuasive language, and tailoring your image to fit the needs of the media. They know what works and doesn't. But, most important, publicists have contacts and can open doors that you may not be able to—including reporters, editors, radio station hosts, and influential blogs. On the downside, if you have a very specialized business or aesthetic, they might not be able to articulate your products as well as you can. If it's not the right fit, they can also become a barrier preventing you from making a personal connection with the media. And publicity also comes with a price—usually the cost of a salaried employee, anywhere from $1,000 to $5,000 per month.

ADVERTISING

While publicity is free (and what small-business owner doesn't love that word), you don't have any control over the message. Despite giving the reporter an angle, you can't dictate how he will ultimately portray your business in the newspaper. We have been misquoted or misrepresented in articles (a newspaper article once said Meg owned a crafts supply business and Cat was a wedding planner—both untrue). It happens. A writer will misunderstand what a subject has said or will be in a hurry to meet a deadline, or the publisher just doesn't do any fact-checking. All this illustrates the ultimate perk of advertising: You are in control of the message.

There are two ways to look at advertising—you can wage an "image campaign," which is about increasing your market's awareness of your company; it's mostly about brand and name recognition. It only works through repetition—that is, you have to repeatedly put your name out there, so your company becomes the first thing that comes to mind when people think of vintage housewares. When the time comes for someone to redecorate her house, she will go directly to your business. Image campaigns should be planned efforts that utilize a set of ads that have a consistent look or message. It's best spread over a variety of media, such as print advertising in magazines and banner ads on blogs or Web sites. True, repetition can cost money and be expensive—but just running an advertisement once or twice may not be helpful at all.

The second type of campaign is not about brand recognition but is meant to push a product, service, or event—like a clearance sale on your Web site. These ads can be run for shorter periods leading up to the

 When you choose an advertising campaign, consider your objective first—and what the best medium is for reaching it.

event. Either way, advertising will cost money, so you should employ the help of a graphic designer and possibly even a copywriter to make your ad be as effective as possible. It's important to present visuals that are aesthetically pleasing, with copy that is well written, compelling, and focused on your message, to make your ad dollars worthwhile.

When you choose an advertising campaign, consider your objective first—and what the best medium is for reaching it. Because ad dollars are precious, pick the best time for placement for your industry or product. For example, if you are coming out with a necklace featuring a pendant with inspirational verses, you may want to consider the holiday season or Valentine's Day issue of a magazine.

For creative businesses starting out, Web advertising will likely be the most affordable option. Think about where you spend your time online; your customers are probably a lot like you and can be found in places that you frequent. Contact each site to see what their reach is like and if you can afford their ad rates. You can track which ads are generating the most responses and pushing the most traffic to your site by putting a "How did you hear about us?" field in your mailing list sign-up form or shopping cart. Alternatively, you can use a service like DoubleClick Ad Planner to help you determine which of your ads are the most effective. Advertising is a guess-and-check game, and over time you'll find the best places for your ad campaigns.

MAKE YOUR MARKETING PLAN

There are so many options when it comes to marketing—we've touched on some of the major ones here. Throughout the life of your business, you should put together a marketing plan at the start of every quarter. Depending on your goals and budget each quarter and the stage of your business, you should gauge the appropriateness of one marketing tactic over others. Don't do a scattershot approach and just engage in marketing when you need it (i.e., when business is slow).

Your marketing plan can consist of something as simple as a calendar plotted with dates when you intend to launch marketing campaigns. You may want to do an e-mail blast advertising the clearance sale on your online gift shop right before the holidays or send out a press release for a new product right before you attend a trade show. Setting target dates is one of the surefire ways to keep you from sliding on your marketing. Despite the importance of marketing, it tends to be one of the first tasks to fall off a small-business owner's to-do list. The trick is to turn something you *should* do into something you *do*. So make a habit out of working on your marketing at least once a week for a couple of hours—pick a day of the week and do it. Keep it up for at least a month and it will become a routine.

SAVOR

Bath and Body Products
Concord, California

Almond Biscotti. Marshallow Fudge. Ginger Crumbcake. With delectable names like that, you'd think Lisa Salamida was running a pastry shop. In actuality, they're the names of soaps she makes for her Etsy-run shop, Savor. Within the first three months of launching it, signs of progress were apparent everywhere in the home she shared with her husband, Mike. The kitchen was no longer an area to prepare or cook meals, but a place for creating and packaging soaps. And no wonder—she had received more than one thousand sales orders in that brief period of time. Pretty good for someone who had opened an Etsy shop simply to get rid of her excess soap projects. With the birth of her daughter, Rowan, in 2010, she quit her full-time job as an editor to focus on her business and care for her child. After only four years of operation, Lisa's company is poised as one of the top Etsy handmade sellers with more than 23,000 sales—showing how a mix of both serendipity and a keen observation of the market can make your company an overnight success.

How did you get started making soaps?

In 2000, I moved to San Francisco to become an editor at a newswire. I didn't know anyone when I moved here, so I made soaps as a hobby to occupy my time. I learned by reading and watching tutorials online. I ended up making too many soaps—and there's just so much you can give away to coworkers or family. My apartment was filling up so I just stopped making them.

What made you decide to start an Etsy storefront?

In 2007, my husband, Mike, who at the time was also an editor at the newswire, made some prints of his paintings and put them up on Etsy. He actually sold quite a few. I thought: Why not open a shop on Etsy to get rid of some soaps? I put about thirty soaps on my store and sold some the very next day. I was hooked!

 What do you think contributed to your early success?

When I opened my Etsy store, it was at the end of October—prime holiday season. The timing was perfect; I just didn't realize it. Sales exploded almost immediately—multiple orders daily were pretty common. I got a business license right away because I figured out immediately that this was going to be real.

On Etsy, there are thousands of shops—and every day another shop with good pictures and good products appears. You can list as many items as you possibly can, but in the end you're still counting on chance foot traffic to arrive. So within that first month, I bought an online ad. It was a holiday ad that offered a small discount. I took a look at where I like to spend my time online—and I decided to place an ad on a site that had nothing to do with craft; it was actually a site where people discussed news links! I figured that if I liked to go there, there must be other people like me with similar interests. The ad helped generate much of my early business. I think crafters tend to put ads up on sites that are frequented by other Etsy artists—but your ad will just get lost among others that are selling something similar. I still buy ad space about two to three times a year, but I do them all on sites that are not Etsy-oriented in any way.

 It's exciting to launch something and get such an immense response. What were the first few months like?

It was wonderful but awful. At the time, my husband and I lived in Walnut Creek but we were still working in San Francisco. We had a two-hour commute every day. When we'd get home from work, we still had to make soap to fill orders. We were working eighty-hour weeks with only the two of us doing it all. At the time, we had a small two-bedroom condo—and the entire place was taken over by soap. The kitchen was devoted to making soap, so we ate out a lot. The only room that didn't have soap was our bedroom.

How did you come up with the name Savor?

I remembered a story about how George Eastman came up with the name Kodak: He basically wanted a business name that was simple to say. So I started brainstorming for short, easy-to-remember names. Since my soaps have a foodie element to them, Savor was the one that stuck.

What changes did you have to make with your business when you became a mother in 2010?

I had to shut down the business a week before and a week after my delivery date. I had been doing this business for four years on the side and it was an immense amount of work. So when Rowan was six months old, I decided to quit my full-time job and work on my business. Currently, everything is still done by me. I work on the business when my daughter is in day care for two hours each morning about three days a week and during the weekends when Mike is home. It's really difficult to do anything when Rowan's around, especially when I'm making soap. Now that she's older, she's more mobile and wants to be entertained all the time.

Aside from having good images or good descriptions for their products, do you have any tips for new Etsy sellers?

I see a lot of people on Etsy forums complaining about their lack of sales—and then I visit their storefront and they have ten items to sell. No wonder no one is buying anything—it's an empty store! You have to have at least twenty different items; that way people have a selection and they can find something that they'd like to get.

surviving THE JUGGLE

Picture the first phone conversation when we discussed writing this book: our voices strained trying to speak into our cell phones over the background noises, including Meg's eight-year-old crying because she had run into a table, Cat's eighteen-month-old throwing purée on their Boston terrier, and our land lines ringing with probably our partner or assistant on the opposite ends. All that was missing was a pot boiling over on the stove to make it a classic chaotic-mom movie scene. Welcome to the juggle. As you can see, it's not always easy PURSUING ENTREPRENEURIAL DREAMS AND MOTHERHOOD. Despite the domestic and business chaos that comes with it, there is not a mom in this book who would want to give up her business and the lifestyle that comes with it. There is an INEXPRESSIBLE REWARD to being able to find a creative outlet for a living. This chapter will show you HOW TO SURVIVE everything in between the highs and lows while satisfying and BALANCING THE DEMANDS OF A GROWING BUSINESS and a burgeoning home life.

Shift by shift, like a nursing-meets-circus rotation at the hospital, is how a majority of mom entrepreneurs get through their day. When we plan our days, we've found that it's much easier to divide the day into shifts and to plan accordingly. If this is your first foray into such a schedule, this is how it might typically play out.

Morning shift: It's the changing of the guard. A typical morning shift has the requisite tasks of getting the kids up, dressed, fed, and ready for school or the sitter. If you've got the energy, you can squeeze in a few business tasks before they wake, such as correspondence, checking for incoming orders, shooting off a quick tweet, and maybe even making a short phone call. It's probably not good to do this once they wake up since the start-stop aspect of putting the jacket sleeve on your child while hitting send on an e-mail can be too chaotic; plus, you might get so carried away with work that you'll cause your child to be late for school. Not good. We've also learned to abstain from any designing, crafting, or other attention-intensive tasks in this harried window.

Midday shift: Once you've returned home from shuttling the kids or the nanny has arrived, you'll finally have some solitude—this is when time is precious and you need to milk every second of it. We've found that it's best to "warm up" by first tackling any e-mail or administrative tasks in the first hour. Next, pull out the to-do list and jump into your priorities. This is the best shift for time-intensive tasks such as designing or crafting, meeting with vendors or clients, or doing a string of blog posts for the week. If you're able to check off a chunk of your to-do's, you might even squeeze in some grocery shopping or a drop-off at the dry cleaners at the tail end of this shift.

Late-afternoon shift: Many moms choose to unplug, as in put away the laptop and the iPhone, at this time and put the off-duty sign up. This shift is all about high-quality one-on-one time with your children: catching up on what happened at school, sitting down to help them with their homework, running their bath, and making dinner.

Evening shift: After you've put the little ones to bed and maybe even clocked in time with your spouse or significant other, another precious window of time opens up. You've known and utilized this shift ever since your little ones were infants. You concocted their Halloween costumes or cranked out craft projects in this twilight hour. Since it's so reliably quiet, this is when Cat spends time designing and illustrating stationery products. Real creative work can be done at this time with the help of a little caffeine and some chocolate.

FINDING BALANCE

It would be a minor miracle not to experience stress from days spent filling out orders while managing work deadlines and parenting shifts that piggyback on each other. Not to mention the pressures of modern-day motherhood can be overwhelming. There are many ways to combat stress, prevention being foremost as well as the realization that you can't be in three places at once. With such time constraints, finding balance also requires a little more strategy and planning. Consider actively working these practices into your weekly routine:

No. 1 TAKE A TIME-OUT

Yes, even adults need them—in a good way. If you're working from home, actually stepping away from work briefly and periodically to walk around the block or paint your toenails on the deck can actually help recharge you and put you in a better mood. You'll return ready to dive into work with your creative juices flowing.

No. 2 ORGANIZE YOUR MOTHERSHIP

Start by centralizing some of the tasks that you find yourself doing each day. If you blog, tweet, and post on Facebook, consider managing those applications in one place like the social media dashboard HootSuite. The same goes for your to-do lists as well as syncing family and work calendars; we use Google and Yahoo! Calendars and Scrybe.

No. 3 RESPOND QUICKLY

Make it a practice to answer your e-mail and return messages as soon as you can. This is a tried-and-true tip from bloggers who often field hundreds of e-mail messages within the span of a day. There is nothing like the buildup of correspondence that can turn downright unmanageable if left neglected.

No. 4 EAT HEALTHFULLY

Working at home has its vices, especially when the kitchen is within a few feet of where you are working. To combat junk food snacking, stash healthful energy snacks like almonds, fruit, and yogurt.

No. 5 DON'T FORGET TO SLEEP

Although evenings are invaluable for moms to design and create, there is a price for overindulging in too many late nights. Sleep deprivation can wreak havoc on your body, your mind, and the quality of your work and time with your little ones. Prioritize getting some solid hours of sleep on a regular basis and try to squeeze in some power naps whenever you can. It may also help to front-load your sleep (that is, sleep before 10:00 P.M.) and wake up by 5:00 A.M. to begin your day's "morning shift."

Motherhood isn't about sainthood. You don't have to grow your own vegetables and purée them for your newborn, if you'd rather buy available healthful options. And you shouldn't feel bad if you have put your child in front of the television for a short while so that you can finish the dishes—everyone does it. Do what works for you and your family and don't beat yourself up with comparisons.

DEALING WITH MOM GUILT

You've been so busy with your business that you asked the sitter to watch your child all day. Meanwhile your sink's piled high with dirty dishes and your response to the question "What's for dinner?" is take-out— again. Welcome to the tortured mind of a guilt-ridden mother. First off, it is not your moral duty and obligation to cook, clean, *and* do child care. You're not a pathetic excuse for a mother—you're simply a busy mother dealing with the side effects of launching a business! There will be days when you are working on a deadline and might not be able to spend time with your daughter. Other days, fulfilling jewelry orders might have to take a backseat to playing with the kids during a snow day. Take it easy on yourself. If you're filled with a gut-wrenching feeling at the thought of leaving your child under someone else's supervision, find someone who is kind toward your child, trustworthy, and reliable to soften any guilty feelings. And the fact that you don't have the time to do everything doesn't take away from the things you do for your family and business. Short-circuit your feelings of guilt, and you'll be happier and more productive.

Two main reasons we moms have such disdain for and guilt about saying no are that (1) our nurture button goes off whenever someone asks for assistance, and (2) it feels like it will be easier to acquiesce than hurt someone's feelings or lose out on a potential opportunity. Instead of thinking of it as outright rejection, change your perception: Saying no is essential to your business's progress. Say no to projects that you don't have time for, that aren't a good fit with your aesthetic, or whose budget isn't ample enough. You have to edit your priorities and streamline your business to stay efficient, not to mention to save your sanity.

Here are some tips to help you deliver that "no" with ease.

- Keep it short. Lengthy explanations about why you can't make fifty button earrings for a charity event are not necessary. It's probably more information than the receiver needs to hear. A genuine and polite "Thank you so much for asking me to, but I am busy at the moment" is all that is needed.

- Stick to your guns. Don't let a people-pleaser attitude get the best of you. Don't feel guilty and waver back and forth about your decision. Remember, you are playing the role of editor—you eliminated a project that wasn't a good fit, so now go out there and find the projects that are complementary to your style!

- Give referrals. One of the hardest parts of saying no is the thought that you might be burning a bridge with someone. You can soften the blow by offering them referrals to other companies that could accommodate their needs.

BONNIE TSANG

Freelance Photography
Los Angeles, California

There is an ethereal and journalistic quality to Bonnie Tsang's photography that her clients clamor for—which may not be surprising, considering that her father was also a photographer. The talent, it would seem, is in Bonnie's blood. However, what is surprising is that Bonnie's start with photography was born more of necessity than of an artistic call. Bonnie was working as an office assistant and going through a divorce when she decided that she would moonlight as a photographer to help support her daughter, Venise. Her love and talent for photography soon became evident and were validated through her Flickr page. Wanting to learn more, she shadowed photographers for a year to acquaint herself with the trade. Since then, her work has been featured on *Daily Candy* and *Southern Weddings*, and in *Martha Stewart's The Bride's Guide*. Admittedly, Bonnie's juggle, which centers on being a single mom, is challenging, but she says it strengthens her belief in family, the rewards of perseverance, and, most important, her bond with her daughter.

 Tell us about your background and how you got into photography.

Photography always felt natural to me. I grew up with photography around me since my dad was a professional photographer. But I didn't really get into it until about seven years ago, when my daughter was born. Just like every mom, I started shooting her. And I continued to shoot whenever I went out, and posted the images on a Flickr account. At that time I was working as an admin with a nine-to-five job. Things really happened when I started Flickr—I met more photographers and developed more of an interest in it. Eventually someone asked if I wanted to shoot their friend's wedding—and it started just like that.

When you look back at your first photos and wedding shoots what do you think?

I think "crappy." In the beginning it was more experimental—let's try this angle; let's try that angle. Eventually, you find your way through to what works and what doesn't work. My first photo on Flickr was actually a picture of a hummingbird and it made it to the top of a Flickr list. Up until that point, I didn't fully realize how much photography could have an effect on people. When I was asked to shoot my first wedding, I just jumped at it. However, after I shot that first wedding, I realized that I should've had more experience before taking on someone's once-in-a-lifetime memory. Even though it turned out great, in hindsight, it was a big responsibility that I probably wasn't yet ready for. So to gain more experience, I started assisting other photographers for a couple of years. I highly recommend working for someone else even if you have to work for free.

What goals do you have as a photographer when working with clients?

As a wedding photographer, I am working to capture someone's memories. As much as I want to do my own thing, I have to remind myself that this is someone's big moment. I can't just feel artsy and shoot someone's back. I'm here to capture a couple's happiest moments. My customers' memories outweigh my identity as a creative artist. I always tell other photographers who want to get into wedding photography not to look at wedding photos, because they're usually very "wedding-y." I would suggest that they look at editorial magazines like *Vogue* or *Travel + Leisure*.

During an appointment I sit down and show clients my process, my vision. But after that I try to listen as much as I can without interrupting them. I want to know what they want, what they are looking for, what kind of styles they are interested in. I usually bring one of my albums as well to show them my layout.

Q *Does being a single mom and being a photographer ever conflict?*

It's funny—I started photography because I was going through a divorce and I was trying to figure things out with my ex-husband. Though he was going to provide child support, I still felt like it was my responsibility to make sure that my daughter was taken care of. Working as an admin wasn't going to be enough for us to have a comfortable life. I felt like I needed a second job and jumped into wedding photography. Little did I know that it would turn into a full-time job that would allow me to quit my admin job. But during the transition, it was a lot of work. That whole year was so challenging because I didn't have enough time with my daughter. I was struggling with "How am I going to pursue photography with a full-time job and being a full-time mom?" I felt bad asking for help. But in the end I did reach out and everyone was so willing. I think for every mom, asking for help is the number-one thing; don't be afraid to ask for it! Being a single mom doesn't mean you have to suffer. I learned that no matter your situation you can enjoy life with your kids without suffering. As a single mom, I admire married moms for having to balance so many roles. You could say I have one less!

Q *How do you juggle your day?*

After my divorce, I couldn't balance for the longest time. On top of taking care of my daughter, I was also living with my parents, and taking care of them, too. Like many moms, I wasn't sleeping because once my daughter went to sleep I would start working. The next day you're so tired that you're grumpy. And if your kid is not listening to you, you get even more cranky and guilty. But one day I figured this whole balance thing. I realized that family is never part of the "balance," family is what centers you. I've decided that in the morning there's no work, it's always going to be my daughter and breakfast time.

I think a lot of times we rush ourselves, thinking, "How am I going to be able to do all this?" because we feel like we need to compete with other people. But then when you figure it out, there's no competition. The only person you need to compete with is yourself. I think that I am still on that journey.

Finding individuals or a group with common triumphs and tribulations has been such an uplifting and inspiring experience for us. Cat's group of designing moms on her online community, Mom Inc Daily, shares everything from tips on how to exhibit at trade shows to doing a group coloring-book project. Best of all, having a group gives a steady reminder that you are not alone!

Online sites: These provide the least amount of commitment and give you daily doses of articles and perspectives on anything from mompreneurship to parenting tips. Some popular sites such as Babble and Rookie Moms supply unique insights and solace into parenting. Online communities like BlogHer and Café Moms provide groups and forums on anything from pregnancy to social media.

Local groups: Belonging to a local group gives you the advantage of being able to share tips for nearby resources as well as give referrals for vendors on both business and personal levels. It's also a great way to locate care (think nannies, short-term sitters) and play groups. (Cat belongs to Golden Gate Mothers Group.) To find a local group, you can visit sites like Meetup.com that will give you listings based on where you live. You can also visit local children's boutiques to see what's posted on their bulletin boards as well as query the owners, since they often know where the moms are gathering in the neighborhood.

Start your own group: This sounds more labor intensive than it is. Your own group can be as simple as your closest friends or peers coming together for coffee to regularly share, vent, or powwow over specifically themed subjects like creating press kits or sharing vendor sources.

Time for *moi*? This probably sounds completely foreign to you. While the moms in this book admit that they don't have oodles of time for themselves, they still make sure to devote an hour here and there to have brunch with friends, get a manicure, or go for a haircut. Cat's secret weapon is investing a few hours a week to hit the gym in the morning before heading to her studio. In fact, the tighter her project deadlines, the more she works out, because it provides extra energy and mental clarity. Meg schedules monthly lunches with her girlfriends. The key is to schedule your "me time" and put it on the calendar, like you would for your child's ballet class. Although solitude, exercise, and interaction with friends may cut into your work time, it provides the balance, sustenance, and inspiration you need for your personal and creative lives.

STORK DELIVERY

If you're expecting a baby, you may be wondering how you will manage bonding with your newborn or adjusting to motherhood while you keep the business operational. If you plan carefully in the months leading up to your delivery, you can keep your business going; take action to ensure your clients, customers, or readers will still be there when you return; and even take a maternity leave to spend time with your new child.

Six to Eight Months Before Baby

Outline a realistic maternity leave plan detailing how much time you can afford to take off and how you plan to run the business during this time. You shouldn't plan to work up until the day of your delivery; build in a couple weeks to relax before childbirth and at least a month afterward to physically and mentally recuperate and bond with your newborn. The type of business you have will ultimately determine the total time you can realistically take off. With blogging, you probably don't want to go too long without posting—and your pregnancy and birthing experience may even be good fodder for your posts. With service-based businesses, you should schedule your projects to end before your delivery and new projects to begin when you're ready. Using your discretion, feel free to let some of your clients know that you are pregnant as a way to give them advance notice on your impending maternity leave, especially if you'll be closing the office for a period of time. Product and retail businesses are the least flexible regarding shutting down temporarily, because you will still need to ship out orders if they come in. This makes hiring someone temporarily to fill orders and handle the day-to-day business matters more important.

Three to Five Months Before Baby

If you provide a service such as photography or graphic design, stop recruiting new business—and wait until after the baby arrives to add new projects or clients. With online retail, unless your child's arrival coincides with the holidays or another major sales day, hold off on adding new inventory to your site until after your child arrives. For now, you should concentrate on maintaining your existing workload, selling existing inventory, and completing any ongoing projects. If you're looking to hire someone temporarily, begin your search now and consider what tasks can be delegated to the person you hire. At home, you may want to look into hiring temporary household help as well if you can afford it.

One to Two Months Before Baby

Be sure to tell your clients or vendors that you'll be on maternity leave and for how long. If you've decided to hire someone, let your clients know that a dependable staff person will be taking care of their needs if they need to speak to someone in your absence. Make sure you train your new staff person or intern well so that you can be assured that your business will be in good hands. Create your "away" message once you've officially gone on maternity leave—note that you will be checking your messages intermittently and provide the name of a contact person, if any, for immediate needs.

After the Baby Arrives

You'll be dealing with postpartum exhaustion, so this isn't the time to dive right back into the business. Try to stay off your feet and give yourself time to recuperate, sleep, and get your energy back. If you have family members and friends asking what they can do to help, have them do household chores or make meals for you. When you're done with maternity leave, be sure to send an e-mail to your clients (possibly with a baby announcement, if that feels right) to let them know you are back and excited to work with them again.

SIBLINGS

If you envision your children swapping toys peacefully and helping each other with chores so that you can get work done, think again. In our experience, they're more likely to swap punches than toys. If you're at home with your children while you're working, you can't spend much time refereeing sibling squabbles. And, as inclined as you might be to give your older child more responsibilities, don't expect too much from her. She won't be able to fill your shoes when it comes to discipline. If you can, find individual activities for each child that relegate them to their own corner of a room so that you can get some quiet time. Better yet, hire a sitter to keep your kids happy and busy while you're working.

SYLVIA WEINSTOCK CAKES

Cake Design
New York, New York

At eighty years young, Sylvia Weinstock has achieved legendary status as the "Queen of Cakes." Working from her bustling studio in Tribeca, she still has her finger on the pulse of her business—from checking in on individual orders and inspecting whether an artist has properly thinned up the arms of a ballerina figurine to fielding calls from New York's elite. You might think Sylvia's pedigree included training at Le Cordon Bleu, but in actuality she was first a schoolteacher and mother of three. Looking for a fresh start, she asked retired pastry chef George Keller if she could learn his techniques. With the skills she learned from him, she got her big break when a friend put her intricately designed cake in the window of a catering shop. Since then she has blazed the trail, putting artistry and exacting quality in both technique and taste in cakes. In addition to being widely published in the press, she counts luminaries such as Donald Trump, Oprah Winfrey, Mariah Carey and the Saudi royal family among her clients.

You don't have any formal training in pastry, yet you had renowned Chef Keller place so much trust in you. What do you think it was that made him willing to take a chance on you?

I had a passion for what I was doing and I understood perfection. I also love good food. When you get that combination together, people can relate to it, and they are perfectly willing to give you some help. Having a dream is just a part of the puzzle. You could dream to be an opera singer and you might have a decent voice, but unless you have that special quality, you don't rise to the Metropolitan Opera House. It's the same sort of thing. You have to have a realistic point of view of what your talent is. I'm meeting a lot of people who say that they want to be cake decorators, but they really can't bake. They're not artists. They're in love with this idea of cake decorating, but they don't know what it means. Can you create the "something" to put on the cake? Is there a skill in just poking a hole into something? Do you have an eye for color and balance? You have to become familiar with all of this.

Q *What do you value in your cakes and your customer service?*

We are very detailed. Food quality is very important. What goes into my body has to be the best. I don't like food dyes or chemicals. I like everything pure and clean. We have a standard of quality where there are no shortcuts. Just like in life. My business has a mission statement about our quality: If you settle for less, you get less. I get emotionally involved with the whole process and absorb it all. We make sure the client gets personalized treatment. We communicate on a personal level: I like to know how she met him, what she does for work, what he does for work, what the family is like, what her dream is, where they are going for a honeymoon, what her vision for the whole thing is about. I can't dictate to her what she'll eat. She's going to have to tell me what her thoughts are, and we'll work it out together. Nobody wants somebody telling you what you have to do.

Q *Your work ethic is legendary. Even in your personal life. You were struck with breast cancer but you fought it so valiantly, saying your reward for this life has come from working so hard and battling through the illness.*

In this business, I was so concerned with what I was producing for a client that I had no time to have headaches or to feel sorry for myself. I was able to take that energy and put it into a product. And I think most people will understand that if you are going to sit around and be sorry for yourself, it's just exasperating. If you could do something and not think about it, it would translate into more energy—positive energy.

How have you parlayed your skills as a schoolteacher and mother into your business?

You will carry the skills you learn as a schoolteacher for the rest of your life. I learned to be patient, to not lose my temper. As a mother you gain warmth and learn how to be very nurturing. I could knit, needlepoint, and garden. I sewed the kids' clothes when we were young and couldn't afford clothes. I also liked to entertain and create a home—and that's where the dessert business came in. Of course, I am a wife. I married a young man who was an attorney. Some husbands are threatened by ambitious and smart wives. But I am fortunate to have a wonderful husband. Looking back, we both understood how creativity was important in our lives, so we fostered that with each other and in our family.

 When you were growing your business, how did you approach funding and finances?

My husband and I are rather frugal. Before Anastasia, my assistant, I had a young woman who worked for me and there were two checks that would go to Con Edison. She would put them in two envelopes with two stamps. I said to her, "Why don't you put both checks in one envelope since they're going to the same address?" When I was learning the business with Mr. Keller—a Frenchman who had lived during the Second World War—when he would use milk, he would turn it upside down and let it sit for a while because it always gave a quarter of a cup more just to get to the last drop. He would do the same when he cracked eggs; he would always scoop it out. We are a wasteful society. We put too much food on the table, and we don't eat it. We throw it out. The answer is to save.

 It's hard to put a price on art, but how do you figure out your fees?

I try to figure out how many hours a cake is going to take to make and figure out which "hands" will be doing it. We have it divided so that certain ladies make certain flowers. I know pretty much how many flowers they can make a week, and include their salary and all the other things to try to figure out what the flowers are worth. I said to one of the artists making figurines the other day, "How long did it take you to do that?" I wanted to figure her salary and everything else so we'd know whether we're charging enough money for this. Frequently, we're not.

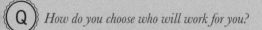

Q *How do you choose who will work for you?*

In my staff, I look for dedication: someone who is detail oriented, pleasant, not moody, and good on the phone. In the back room, I look for people who have good hand skills because we can teach them from there. Artists have a lot of patience and an eye for detail, as well as skill. When they come in I give them a little trial period: make me an animal, make me a figurine. Let's see how good you are at it. They also need to have reasonably cool hands, because hot hands won't work.

Q *Do you ever feel creatively burned out? What do you do about it? What do you do for yourself?*

Drink vodka. Every once in a while I say, "I hate my life," and sit down and have a drink, but that's few and far between. I go out to lunch every now and then. I get my hair cut, which is a wonderful hour. This business is totally consuming. You can wake up in the middle of the night with a thought. You're on tap all the time. You're making something for a moment in people's lives that is very critical, so you are always concerned that they be satisfied and happy. That's your reputation, your word of mouth. You walk down the street and run into someone whose wedding cake you made and they'll say, "You did our wedding cake ten years ago; it was so wonderful."

Q *Do you have any advice for someone who wants to get into the cake decorating business?*

Don't ever think you're a diva; you're in the service business. You have to please someone and it's all done for the business. Once you get an attitude and think you're a hot shot, things go awry.

HIRING STAFF

When you feel the crunch of progress in your business, sometimes it means that you've gone as far as you can on your own engine. It may be time to start hiring help. This isn't a decision to take lightly—you'll have to pay them, delegate tasks and dictate their workload, share your office space with them, and provide them with the tools (like a computer) to carry out their tasks. On the upside, having additional help can increase productivity and allow you to focus on the tasks you're best at. When you think

 You should look for someone with whom you have a good rapport; someone who is responsible (shows up on time), eager to learn, and believes in your business and genuinely wants to help it grow.

about the person you need and the skills they require, consider creating a position that includes tasks you don't enjoy doing or don't have the patience or aptitude for (perhaps it's bookkeeping or packaging orders). Consider as well how much you should pay this person and how you will budget for it. As with any small businesses, it's hard to compensate someone properly for what they're actually worth. You may want to start out with recent college graduates or unpaid interns.

An intern is usually someone who is still in college or fresh out of school, often with little real-world experience. Internships are often a part-time and temporary employment arrangement—typically, interns spend about 10 to 20 hours a week in your office for a limited period, like three or four months. They may be looking for studio experience or the chance to see how a creative operation functions. More than likely, there will be a lot of hand-holding involved. You should start interns off with basic responsibilities, for example, cutting sheets of parchment paper, sticking labels on products, or tagging images in blog posts—so find someone who won't be bored by this but rather will find this to be a learning experience. Don't expect too much of your intern initially, like asking them to tweet on your behalf, take client appointments, or be the point of contact for company e-mails. They may eventually get there, but it could take months, or even the full internship period, before they are attuned to your company's mission and aesthetic. On the plus side, they can be a low-paying or free source of talent (you can arrange for them to receive a small stipend or school credit if they're in school) and may be open to a less-traditional work environment (a.k.a. your home). Internships can also be a good way to test out an employee before bringing her on as an entry-level hire.

If you're looking for an assistant, look for one with the attributes of a rock-star intern (or even better, turn your best intern into your assistant) but with more finessed technical skills. Does she possess skills to update the HTML coding on your blog? Does she have iron-clad bedside manners toward clients or customers? If you are not present, can she command respect from your flour and fondant vendors? Unlike an intern who might be given more leeway with any mistakes they may make, assistants for creative businesses are expected to be responsible, competent, and a bit of a self-starter to assist with running the day-to-day operations.

When you post a job or an internship, be as detailed as possible, including the tasks they'll be responsible for as well as the duration of the internship. Getting the right employee will require you to check résumés and references as well as do some online reconnaissance like checking their Facebook page and blogs. (People tend to reveal a lot about themselves online.) When you interview a potential candidate, be up front about what it's like to work for you. Will they be okay with a noisy work space—that is, one where your kids might be playing or occasionally spatting in the background? Include a brief rundown of your work environment and encourage them to be candid about their comfort with it.

As business owners we are all looking for the same type of employee: intelligent, outgoing, friendly, and loyal with the work ethic of an Oompa Loompa, but it may be hard to find someone who embodies all those qualities. You should look for someone with whom you have a good rapport; someone who is responsible (shows up on time), eager to learn, and believes in your business and genuinely wants to help it grow.

You've been accustomed to the low overhead and rent as well as being the sole employee, but there are times when a business has crossed a threshold and success can only be sustained if you encourage its growth. If you're experiencing any of the following growth signs, take it as a cue to review your business needs for a larger space, employees, or outsourcing.

- The majority of your day is spent on packaging orders, fielding inquiries from customers, or tackling administrative tasks like invoicing. Subsequently, you hardly have enough time to spend designing or generating new project ideas.

- There is no longer space for your son's hockey gear because your garage is filled to the gills with packaged onesies waiting to get shipped to customers.

- The three-year goals in your business plan have been accomplished in less than half the time.

- Clients you would love to work with are now being turned away because of scheduling conflicts.

- The demands of the business have swelled to a point that you are no longer feeling creative or motivated.

Without a doubt, one of the great rewards of having a creative business is that your family will bear witness to all of your endeavors. It also naturally lends itself to something children can relate or even contribute to in small ways. The great payoff to this is that you have their involvement and understanding (if not appreciation)—seeing how hard mom

 Being your own boss allows you to bend the rules a little and involve your family in as many or as few ways as you desire.

works shows them your responsibility, dedication, and sense of pride in one's accomplishments. If you have little helpers, letting them cut ribbon for a package or stuff cards into cellophane bags are ways in which they can be involved and spend some quality time with you. On occasion, many of the moms in this book have taken their children to craft fairs, photo shoots, and vendor field trips. If your daughter loves playing dress-up, she can be the fit model for your handmade aprons. If the family likes cooking together, they can be the taste testers for your experimental batches of salted caramels. Being your own boss allows you to bend the rules a little and involve your family in as many or as few ways as you desire. But you might also find yourself challenged by the good and the bad of a growing business and family. As you get busier and find yourself in the middle of a juggle, it's good to keep in mind the perks: being able to stay in your pajamas until eleven o'clock in the morning, having full control over the scheduling of your day, and being able to call off work at a moment's notice to play a board game with the kids.

For more information on the interviewees featured in the book:

Agatha Achindu/Yummy Spoonfuls, *www.yummyspoonfuls.com*
Amy Atlas/Amy Atlas Events, *www.amyatlas.com*
Gabrielle Blair/Design Mom, *www.designmom.com*
Ellen Diamant/Skip Hop, *www.skiphop.com*
Kelle Hampton/Enjoying the Small Things, *www.kellehampton.com*
Abby Larson/Style Me Pretty, *www.stylemepretty.com*
Christiane Lemieux/DwellStudio, *www.dwellstudio.com*
Janet Morales/Three Potato Four, *www.threepotatofourshop.com*
Cortney Novogratz/Sixx Design, *www.sixxdesign.com*
Cynthia Rowley/Cynthia Rowley, *www.cynthiarowley.com*
Lisa Salamida/Savor, *savor.etsy.com*
Carina Schott/Nonchalant Mom, *www.nonchalantmom.com*
Lorena Siminovich/Petit Collage, *www.petitcollage.com*
Bonnie Tsang/Bonnie Tsang Photography, *www.bonnietsangblog.com*
Sylvia Weinstock/Sylvia Weinstock Cakes, *www.sylviaweinstock.com*

Ad Networks

BlogAds, *www.blogads.com*
Federated Media Publishing, *www.federatedmedia.net*
Glam Media, *www.glammedia.com*
Google AdSense, *www.google.com/adsense*

Blog Hosts

Blogger, *www.blogger.com*
Square Space, *www.squarespace.com*
TypePad, *www.typepad.com*
WordPress, *www.wordpress.org*

Online Resources and Tools

Akismet, *akismet.com*
Cargo Collective, *cargocollective.com*

Cozi, *www.cozi.com*
EcoLogo, *www.ecologo.org*
Evernote, *www.evernote.com*
FFFFOUND!, *www.ffffound.com*
Google Analytics, *www.google.com/analytics*
Google Calendar, *www.google.com/calendar*
Google Keyword Tool, *www.adwords.google.com/select/keywordtoolexternal*
Green Seal, *www.greenseal.org*
Hootsuite, *www.hootsuite.com*
Kickstarter, *www.kickstarter.com*
LogMeIn, *www.logmein.com*
Pinterest, *www.pinterest.com*
QuickBooks, *quickbooks.intuit.com*
Scrybe, *www.iscrybe.com*

Craft Fairs and Retail Shows
Bazaar Bizarre, *www.bazaarbizarre.org*
The Holiday Shops at Bryant Park, *www.theholidayshopsatbryantpark.com*
Renegade Craft Fair, *www.renegadecraft.com*
Urban Craft Uprising, *www.urbancraftuprising.com*
Urban Space Markets, *www.urbanspacenyc.com*

Online Communities
Babble, *www.babble.com*
BlogHer, *www.blogher.com*
Meetup.com, *www.meetup.com*
Rookie Moms, *www.rookiemoms.com*

Organizations
American Institute of Graphic Arts (AIGA), *www.aiga.org*
International Cake Exploration Societe (ICES), *www.ices.org*

Protecting Your Work
Creative Commons, *www.creativecommons.com*
U.S. Copyright Office, *www.copyright.gov*
U.S. Trademark Office, *www.uspto.gov*

Social Media

Facebook, *www.facebook.com*
Flickr, *www.flickr.com*
MySpace, *www.myspace.com*
Twitter, *www.twitter.com*
Vimeo, *www.vimeo.com*
YouTube, *www.youtube.com*

Store Systems, Shopping Carts, and Marketplaces

Authorize.Net, *www.authorize.net*
Big Cartel, *www.bigcartel.com*
Bonanza, *www.bonanza.com*
Etsy, *www.etsy.com*
Homestead, *www.homestead.com*
PayPal, *www.paypal.com*
Shopify, *www.shopify.com*
Supermarket, *www.supermarkethq.com*
Verisign, *www.verisign.com*
Volusion, *www.volusion.com*
Yahoo! Merchant Solutions, *smallbusiness.yahoo.com*

Trade Shows

ABC Kids Expo, *www.theabcshow.com*
American International Toy Fair, *www.toyassociation.org*
Craft & Hobby Association, *www.chashow.com*
George Little Management, *www.glmshows.com*
International Contemporary Furniture Fair, *www.icff.com*
International Gem & Jewelry Show, *www.intergem.com*
MAGIC, *www.magiconline.com*
New York International Gift Fair, *www.nyigf.com*

U.S. Government Resources

Consumer Product Safety Commission, *www.cpsc.gov*
Internal Revenue Service, *www.irs.gov*
U.S. Equal Employment Opportunity Commission, *www.eeoc.gov*
U.S. Small Business Administration, *www.sba.gov*

INDEX

To our editors, Kate Woodrow and Lisa Tauber, and our agent, Stefanie Von Borstel, for your expert guidance and enthusiastic support throughout. Special thanks to all of the amazing moms in this book and for their insight and heartfelt stories as mom entrepreneurs: Agatha Achindu, Amy Atlas, Gabrielle Blair, Ellen Diamant, Kelle Hampton, Abby Larson, Christiane Lemieux, Janet Morales, Cortney Novogratz, Cynthia Rowley, Carina Schott, Lisa Salamida, Lorena Siminovich, Bonnie Tsang, and Sylvia Weinstock. Thank you as well to Danielle Maveal of Etsy and Jory Des Jardins of BlogHer.

Cat: To the "boys" in my life, Jason and Nolan. I could not have made it through my all-nighters without your unconditional love, support, and much-needed comic relief. To my father, for being my cheerleader. And to my mom and grandmother in the sky. Love to you all. Meg, words can't describe how thankful I am for the opportunity to write this with you. It has been an honor and privilege to know someone with such heart and entrepreneurial spirit.

Meg: To Marvin, Lauryn, and Miles, for being such a loving and supportive family. Thank you, Mom and Dad, for everything—especially free child care! To my mom, for being so nurturing and inspiring, setting the bar for motherhood, and showing me how multitasking is done. Cat, we are such kindred spirits—I'm so glad we had the opportunity to work on this project together. Here's to more in the future!